the dodo

# NUBBY'S STORY

The True Story of How One Special Dog Beat the Odds

## BY AUBRE ANDRUS

SCHOLASTIC INC.

P9-DGE-757

Photo credits: Cover: © Lou R Images; Title page: © Lou R Images; Photo insert page 1: © Lou R Images; Photo insert page 2 (top): © Lou R Images; Photo insert page 2 (bottom): © The Dodo; Photo insert page 3: © Lou R Images; Photo insert page 4: © The Dodo; Photo insert pages 5–6: © Lou R Images; Photo insert page 7: © The Dodo; Photo insert page 8: © Lou R Images

ISBN 978-1-338-64510-1

10 9 8 7 6 5 4 3 2 1          20 21 22 23 24

Printed in the U.S.A.    40

First printing 2020

Book design by Veronica Mang

# CONTENTS

# CHAPTER 1

## A DOG IS BORN

**LOU ROBINSON RUSHED AROUND** the house searching frantically for a few items. She grabbed a blanket, a basket, and a jacket. She looked at her cell phone one more time, then picked up her car keys. Her husband, Mark, sat in a comfy chair in front of his computer screen. He was working intently and didn't notice the flurry of activity behind him.

"I'm going to pick up a boxer with two legs," Lou called as she walked past Mark and headed toward the front door.

"Alright," Mark said. He heard the door shut. *Wait, what did she say? A boxer with no legs?* Mark must have misheard his wife.

Lou drove as fast as she could through the roads of rural Texas. She and Mark lived outside of Houston, where the roads weren't very crowded. It was a cold but peaceful January day, and the fresh air allowed her to think more clearly. Just minutes before, she had gotten a text message from a friend of a friend. It was a picture of a little white animal. The first thing that popped into her mind was, *What's going on here?* She immediately called her friend back.

"You gotta get over here quick," the woman had said. "We need your help. Our boxer just had a puppy who doesn't have any front legs."

Lou had only one response: "I'm on my way."

Lou was used to caring for animals. Although her full-time job was as a photographer—and she loved taking portraits of kids, couples, and animals—any free moment she had was spent on her animal rescue organization. It was called W.E.A.R., which stood for Warriors Educate About Rescue. She not only rescued lost or abandoned pets, but she also taught people how they could help prevent pets from ending up in animal shelters or on the streets in the first place. As a longtime animal rescuer, she'd cared for dogs with all kinds of issues, but she was used to broken limbs—not missing limbs.

Lou rang the doorbell, and the door opened almost immediately.

"Thank you for coming so quickly," the woman said. "They're over here."

Lou entered the house and spotted the white mother boxer, the brown dad boxer, and a litter of seven puppies in the corner of the living room. When Lou stepped into the room, the mother was instantly very protective and growled like any mama dog would when a stranger approached her newborn pups. Lou paused to let the mother dog know she was a friend. The puppies were snuggling up to the mom's belly to drink milk. They wiggled and crawled as they fought for a chance to eat, like healthy puppies do. But one puppy was getting left behind. He was all white with the sweetest little pink face and the tiniest ears. From a distance, he didn't look any different than his siblings. But as Lou stepped closer, she realized her friend was right. He had no front legs.

Lou sat on the floor and tried to gain the mother boxer's trust. Once the mama calmed down and seemed comfortable, Lou slowly moved the two-legged pup closer to his mother's tummy so he had a chance to eat. A lot of things were running through Lou's mind: This puppy couldn't compete with his squirmy brothers and sisters. He was going to get wiggled out of the pack over and over again. If he couldn't eat, he wouldn't have a chance. But taking a puppy away from his mother can be traumatic for both the puppy and the mother.

After a couple of hours watching the puppies, Lou and her friend made a decision: Lou had to take home the newborn two-legged pup and care for him.

Lou burst through the front door of her house with a small bundle in her arms. A cold breeze followed behind her.

"Did you say you were going to get a boxer with no legs?" Mark asked.

"No. Two legs," Lou said. She carefully pulled back the fleece blanket and showed Mark who was hiding inside.

"Woo!" Mark said. He scratched his gray mustache and beard, and then placed a hand on his bald head. He couldn't believe what Lou was holding. The little pup was so tiny. He had been born just five hours ago. He weighed less than one pound. And he had only two legs. "What are we going to do?"

# CHAPTER 2

## THE FIRST NIGHT

**WHAT WERE THEY GOING TO DO?**
Well, first Lou was going to panic.

"Here. Do something with him. I have to get stuff ready," Lou said as she handed the tiny bundle to Mark.

Lou found a heating pad and a black fleece blanket, then stacked them in a small wicker basket. She set it on the kitchen countertop. Mark paced around the kitchen with the puppy held gently in his arms. He rocked him and bounced him like a baby because that was all he knew how to do. Mark was tall, which made the puppy in his hands look even smaller.

"We're not puppy people," Mark said. Lou and Mark were dog people, sure, but they had never cared for a puppy this young or this tiny. "I'm familiar with bottle-feeding, but this is a neonatal puppy! What do we do? How do we feed him? *What* do we feed him? How the heck are we going to do this?"

Lou rummaged through the kitchen cabinets and grabbed a baby bottle—but it was the same size as the puppy! It was way too big. "We'll reach out to the rescue community for help," she said. She had never dealt with a flat-out newborn puppy who was less than one day old. Were they bottle-fed the same way as a larger, one-week-old puppy? She needed to find out. She adjusted the headband that was holding back her short, dark-brown hair with one hand as she reached for her phone with the other.

Lou knew a lot of other people who ran animal rescue organizations, and they were always more than willing to help one another when they could. Her friends were sure to have some advice on caring for a pup this young, though she didn't think any of them would know how to care for a dog with only two legs. Lou and Mark would need to research that part on their own. "We need to go to the grocery store and get some raw goat's milk," Lou said. "All dogs can survive on that."

At least she knew that much! Mark gently

placed the pup onto the heated blanket, then grabbed his keys and coat. He stepped out into the cold and jogged toward his truck. He shook his head as he climbed in. It was dark out now. He hoped this puppy would live through the night. This was stressful, but he knew this chaos would be worth it if the little puppy made it. Mark knew that he and Lou were all this puppy had. But most importantly, Mark believed in Lou. And she believed animals are important. She wanted to make a difference, even if it was only one dog at a time. Today she'd answered the call. She always did. And she never hesitated. Mark loved that about her.

Lou had to keep the puppy hydrated while Mark was gone. They were going to need a syringe to feed this little guy. She found one in a drawer and topped it with a syringe tip, then filled it with a bit of water and squeezed it slowly into the puppy's mouth just a little bit at a time. He seemed to like it, which was a relief to Lou. They were going to keep this puppy alive drop by drop.

The puppy was starting to relax. He was thirsty, but tired. Someone was putting liquid in his mouth, which he was thankful for. There had been a lot of loud noises, then a cold breeze, but now it was quiet and he was feeling warm and calm. And tired. So tired.

When Mark returned with the goat's milk, Lou showed him how to feed the pup. First they warmed the goat's milk—not too hot and not too cold—and then fed the puppy with the syringe, squeezing just a little bit of liquid into his mouth at a time. Just like a human baby, the puppy had to be burped afterward. Mark placed his finger on the puppy's chest. Lou was giving him step-by-step directions, which she was reading from messages her dog-rescue friends had sent her.

"Hold him right between the nub and the nubby chicken wing," Lou said. She was describing the two short limbs where the puppy's front legs should have been. They weren't completely missing—but they were very underdeveloped. One was a stump and one was a little bit longer with an elbow-like bend. "Pat and then listen for a burp."

Mark did as he was told and the puppy gave a small burp.

And just like a human baby, the little puppy had to be fed every two hours—even in the middle of the night. It was going to be a long night! Mark was already exhausted. They decided he would head to bed early. Lou planned to stay up late reading so she could do two feedings back-to-back. Then, in the middle of the night, Lou would go to bed and Mark would wake up and take the next two feedings. This way, each of them could hopefully get a four-hour stretch of sleep.

Besides feeding the puppy every two hours, there was one other issue that required constant tending: The heating pad that was warming the puppy's blanket was meant for humans. It automatically shut off after a short period of time for safety reasons. But puppies can't regulate their own body temperature until they are four or five weeks old. They usually stay close to their mothers and their brothers and sisters for warmth. But this puppy obviously couldn't do that. The heating pad was keeping him alive. If it accidentally turned off, the puppy could die. Mark set a timer for one hour and forty-five minutes, so they could make sure that the heating pad stayed warm throughout the night. Both Mark and Lou crossed their fingers.

For the next twenty-four hours, Lou and Mark gave the tiny puppy round-the-clock care. He made it through the first night. Then the second one. This tiny pup may have looked weak, but he clearly wasn't ready to give up. Two days after being born, he was still fighting. It felt like a miracle. But every day that followed was scary for Lou and Mark. This puppy would continue to need all the love and protection he could get. And that fact was about to be made even more clear to them.

Lou's friend called to let her know that she was bringing the rest of the litter into the vet to get checked on. She offered to bring the two-legged puppy in with the rest of his siblings.

Lou was tired. The last two days had been long, and she and Mark had barely slept.

"Thanks for offering, but we'll take him in on our own," she told her friend.

Lou looked at the puppy sleeping peacefully on his heating pad. The sight of him made her heart warm.

A short while later, her phone rang. It was Lou's friend calling again. She should have been busy at the veterinarian's office by now. What could she possibly want?

It turned out that her friend had called about something else—something that hadn't even run through Lou's mind. "If you're not up to taking care of him, the vet said he could put him to sleep."

Lou couldn't believe her ears. She glanced at the little white pup, his pink nose, and pink paws as he slept. He was so helpless, but he had lived two full days. And Lou knew he could live longer with help from her and Mark.

"Why would we want to do that?" Lou asked. "With the exception of what's on the outside, you're looking at a theoretically healthy dog. He's just missing two limbs."

Her mind started spinning. She didn't know if this puppy was perfectly healthy. But there was a chance he was, right? And she was willing to find out. *Why, if someone is willing to give him a chance, would they put this dog to sleep? Just because he's different?* Lou was growing furious.

"Not going to happen," Lou said. "Nubby's now in the rescue program and we'll take it from here." She hung up the phone.

*Who would give up on a puppy just because he needs a little extra care?* she thought. *This puppy isn't a typical puppy, but all he needs is a little more love and time. Different is not disposable.*

Mark gave Lou a hug. Nubby was the perfect name for this little pup. "We'll do everything we can to help Nubby," Mark said to Lou. "I believe in you, and our pack believes in you, too."

# CHAPTER 3

## THE PACK

**NUBBY WASN'T THE ONLY DOG** living with Mark and Lou at Hillcrest Manor, the name they had given to their home. There was Olivia Pig, a white bull terrier mix with spotted ears, who Mark and Lou had rescued in 2012. Olivia loved Mark and followed him wherever he went. She was a very compassionate and motherly dog, even though she had never had puppies of her own. Whenever Olivia Pig heard Nubby make even the tiniest noise, she jumped up and then looked to Lou and Mark as if she was saying, "Well, do something!"

That same year, Mark and Lou had taken in Gracie Macy, the blue heeler with a black spot over her right eye. She was in terrible shape when they first rescued her. It turned out that Gracie had allergy and immune issues that caused her skin to bleed. It took a full year for her skin to get healthy and her gray speckled hair to grow back. Now she followed Lou around like a shadow. She was a "checker." Whenever Lou and Mark were fostering a new animal, Gracie would walk over to the pet, sniff them, check that everything was okay, then go lay down. Sniff, check, lay down. Sniff, check, lay down. That was her routine.

The next year, Maggie May, a white Boston terrier with a long tail, came into their lives. She was skinny, shy, and overbred, which means she had been forced to have a lot of puppies. It took eight months before her stomach stopped drooping. She was a very kind dog, but she wasn't instantly friendly with every pet who entered her home. It took about a month for her to warm up to any new animal. But then she'd become their best friend.

And just last year, Rita Rita had joined the pack. She was a little black Affenpinscher mix who loved hanging out with other dogs and other people. She had become Lou's creative muse: She let Lou take her photo while posing in dog-sized hats and outfits!

She was already super interested in the little puppy, which made sense because she was so friendly. "Rita Rita, she's so nice we say it twice," Lou liked to say. Lou could tell that Rita Rita wanted to cuddle with Nubby immediately.

Rita Rita was small, so she couldn't quite see who was hiding in that basket on the kitchen counter. But every so often she saw Mom holding a tiny white bundle in her arms and feeding it with a little tube. *Who is this little animal? Is he a new friend?* Rita Rita loved making new friends. New dogs often came to their house when they had to be cared for. They were usually scared and sick, but then they'd feel better and play with her. But this was the smallest one she had ever seen. He was just a puppy, and he sure slept a lot. Once he was done being tired, she'd be sure to introduce herself. And maybe lick him.

The other dogs looked on from the living room, curiously glancing at the tiny bundle who had been demanding so much of Mom and Dad's attention for the past two days. Gracie walked by Nubby's basket, checked on him, and then left, which was exactly how Lou and Mark expected her to act. It was her way of saying, "You're good? Okay, cool. I'm going to go lay down now." And the past two days, Maggie had walked right past Nubby without a glance. As usual, she refused to acknowledge any new dog who entered the rescue organization until they had been around for at least four weeks. Lou and Mark sure knew their dogs well.

All of the dogs at Hillcrest Manor had been a part of Lou and Mark's rescue organization. Lou and Mark's job was to help dogs (and sometimes other animals, like goats!) get healthy and find the perfect home. After all, they couldn't possibly keep all the animals they rescued. But these four dogs in particular managed to steal their hearts, and they just had to keep them as part of their "permanent resident program."

Concerns were already running through Lou's head about where they'd find a home for this two-legged puppy when he got stronger. She knew that she couldn't rescue every dog in Texas. That's why her nonprofit was called Warriors Educate About Rescue. The organization focused on not only rescuing, but also educating the public about things like microchipping pets (so they wouldn't get lost) and spaying and neutering dogs (so there are fewer puppies born and therefore fewer dogs in shelters). Education was her number one priority. She liked to say that "In order to change the future, we must teach the present." Maybe she could also teach people that "different was not disposable." Nubby would be a good spokespuppy for that message! But first, she had to focus on keeping him alive.

With four dogs to care for and a rescue organization to run, Lou and Mark's life at Hillcrest Manor had always been super busy. This fifth little dog had certainly made things more complicated. As Nubby's caretakers, it was no secret that their life was going to get even busier. But they wouldn't have it any other way.

"Another poop!" Mark said. He jotted down a note in a journal. He and Lou were keeping track of every time Nubby ate and went to the bathroom. "You never saw two people more excited when poo comes out of a butt," he explained to Nubby.

Nubby made it to three days. And then seven days. Then ten days—and then two weeks. This little pup, who had only two legs and had been taken away from his mother when he was just a few hours old, was doing great.

"You're really going to make it!" Mark said as he patted Nubby's head. Mark and Lou were thrilled that Nubby was thriving, but they had to admit it: They were also exhausted! Despite all the odds, this two-legged pup was getting stronger. However, there was one thing that was worrying Lou as more days passed. She now knew that two-legged dogs are slightly delayed when it comes to hitting certain important puppy milestones. This meant if Nubby didn't reach a milestone on time, she shouldn't be nervous. But she couldn't help but be nervous all the same! "He's got no eyes, Mark!" Lou was sure of it. It had been two weeks. Puppies are born with their eyes closed and it takes a couple of weeks before their eyes open. In theory, Nubby should have opened his eyes by now. Lou didn't mind if Nubby was blind, but she was very protective of the little puppy, and she knew he would already have a lot to overcome. If he was blind, she just wanted to find out as soon as possible so she could start preparing for how best to care for him. The anticipation was driving her crazy.

"He's gonna be fine," Mark said. "Look, you can see his eyes moving behind his closed eyelids. They're moving! He's got them!"

Nubby was sleeping on his back, as he preferred to do, his little pink nose pointed upward. He was eating out of a bottle now. He wiggled, and whined when he wanted more food or a cuddle. He was still tiny, but he was developing just as a puppy should.

Nubby wasn't quite sure what was going on. Everything had been a blur for the past few weeks: Sleep, eat. Sleep, eat. He was feeling stronger. But now he could see brightness. He had opened his eyes for the first time. Just a little bit at first, and then all the way. He could see two smiling faces staring back at him. One was a bald man with glasses and a beard. The other was a lady with short, wild hair and a brightly colored sash tied around her head. They seemed extra happy. They petted him softly. He was glad they were happy. But he was going to close his eyes and go back to sleep now. He was tired, and his blanket was so warm.

Now that Nubby's eyes were open, he had a new favorite game: biting Mark's beard. Mark would hold Nubby in his arms and make growling noises, and Nubby would open and close his puppy jaws on Mark's chin. But he was just a puppy, so it wasn't like his jaws were strong. It was funny, until . . .

"Ow. Ow. Ow!" Mark yelled. Lou started laughing and stopped recording the video she was taking of the two of them playing. This puppy was growing before their eyes. He wasn't quite so weak anymore!

Nubby was also loving the brightly colored chew toys they placed in his bed. He sniffed and tried to scoot forward to lick them. He was using his "nubs" like elbows so he could prop his head up and move forward slightly if he positioned his back legs just right. He even wagged his tail—a real tail wag! That was a big deal for a puppy. Lou and Mark were so proud.

Once Nubby's eyes were opened—and Lou

could confirm that yes, Nubby had eyeballs—she had another concern.

"I think he's deaf, Mark." Lou was sure of it.

Puppies' ears are "closed" when they are born. It takes a few weeks for them to "open" and perk up. It's common for white boxers like Nubby to be deaf. His mother was a deaf white boxer. It wouldn't have been surprising if Nubby was deaf, too, especially because his ears hadn't opened yet. Any little thing out of the ordinary was making Lou concerned, but Mark thought she was overreacting. Lou petted Nubby softly as he lay on his pillow. His sweet face was only growing cuter. They'd keep watching him for signs of deafness, but Nubby had overcome the odds already. Lou knew his fighting spirit would continue on no matter what.

# CHAPTER 4

## NUBBY'S FIRST SCARE

**THERE WAS SO MUCH TO SEE AND** do! Nubby couldn't believe it. There were soft things called toys. And he could bite them and shake them. Especially the monkey. There were hard toys in the shape of bones. He could bite those, too. There were soft things called beds, but he wasn't supposed to bite those.

Mom and Dad said so. He could also climb out of the bed, but he wasn't supposed to do that, either. But sometimes he made a game out of it. If Mom and Dad put him in a bed, he'd try his best to climb out. It was fun!

It had been four weeks. Life at Hillcrest Manor was settling down just a little bit. Nubby had become part of Lou and Mark's daily routine, and the other dogs were getting used to him being around. Nubby had a special space set up in the corner of the living room. It was a large corner of the living room that was covered with a colorful play mat, soft fleece blankets, a dog bed, and toys. It was surrounded by a small black gate that kept Nubby from leaving the area.

He was just a little over three pounds, so the other dogs were very careful around him. Rita Rita and Olivia Pig knew to play gently with him, and Olivia Pig even liked to lick his head. Mark and Lou were proud of how well behaved their other pups were. When Olivia Pig accidentally got a little too close to him when she rolled onto her back, Nubby gave a little growl. He even knew how to roll onto his back legs to kick a little when Rita Rita wanted to play-wrestle with him. He was learning to protect himself despite being so small. And, as usual, Gracie was acting as the disciplinarian. If any dog got out of line, she would walk by and give them a look that said, "Hey, you: Behave!" Maggie continued her typical behavior: Pay no attention to the new puppy.

"Maggie, come look!" Lou said, for what

felt like the one hundredth time. As usual, Maggie's body language seemed to say, "I'm going to pretend he's not in the house." Other days, she seemed to give Nubby a look that said, "Who the heck are you?" or "Yeah, I'm not dealing with that." But Lou knew that Maggie would eventually open up. It had been a full month with Nubby, and Maggie couldn't keep ignoring him.

Maggie walked past Nubby, but this time instead of stopping and turning the other direction, she paused and gave him a look. She cocked her head to the side. This little white fur ball had demanded all of her owners' attention for the past month. Every time he wiggled and tried to move, Lou and Mark were thrilled.

And he was still here, four weeks later. *Okay, I guess this one is going to stay around awhile*, she thought as she looked from Nubby to Lou. *I guess I can be his friend.* Nubby was sitting in the corner of the room on a black-and-blue camouflage fleece blanket. Maggie sat down next to Nubby on a light-purple fleece blanket with a monkey print. She looked at the puppy again. This time something didn't look right. The little puppy didn't feel well, she could tell.

Besides worrying about Nubby's challenges, Lou and Mark treated him the same way they treated any other dog. He just didn't have front legs. But today, Lou felt that something was off. She could tell that Maggie had noticed, too.

"Mark! Something's not right," Lou called over her shoulder. Mark came running and looked at the little white puppy who was usually full of energy.

"He's doing good," Mark said. Nubby looked the same. Maybe he was moving less than usual, but he was probably just tired. "He's still a happy little guy."

"No, something's not right." Lou stared at Nubby. When she offered him food, he didn't want it. She convinced him to take a few little nibbles, but it didn't sit well with him. Nubby threw up.

"He's 'urping,' Mark. I'm calling the vet."

Mark gave the pup another look. Even though he seemed happy, it was becoming clear that this puppy was sick.

Lou picked up the phone and explained to

the vet that her little puppy wasn't moving or eating much and that he was urping. *Urping* was a word Lou and Mark used to describe what happened when Nubby spit up his food shortly after eating it. He had urped before. It was something that Lou and Mark were concerned about.

When dogs or cats are bottle-fed, there is a chance they will get aspiration pneumonia. It means that if they choke or vomit too often, their lungs can get inflamed or swollen. It can make swallowing and breathing more difficult.

Nubby was tired again. But he wasn't tired from playing with the other dogs or with his toys. This was a different kind of tired. His throat hurt and his stomach was upset. He felt weak.

He didn't want to move his legs. Not even a little. Usually he was so comfortable on his warm blanket, but even that didn't feel great right now. The white dog named Maggie was sitting next to him, which was nice. She looked kind of like him, but different. Bigger. Hopefully she would go get Mom and Dad. They always knew how to make him feel better.

The veterinarian on the phone was concerned. So was Lou. She rushed Nubby out to the car—at this point, he wasn't moving at all. Now Lou was really scared. She stepped on the gas and backed out of her driveway and onto the road.

*We're going to help you, Nubby. Just hang in there*, she thought as she drove as fast as she could. She arrived at the veterinarian's office quickly, and Nubby was able to get his blood checked immediately. Lou paced in the waiting room. Soon, the vet returned.

"He's not doing well," the vet said. "I think he has pneumonia and you need to get him to the animal hospital in Houston immediately." Lou picked up Nubby. He was still so small and helpless. "I'm calling them right now and letting them know you're on your way."

"I'll get there as fast as I can," Lou said.

Lou hopped back into the car with Nubby and took off for Houston. Forty-five minutes later, she was bursting through the doors of the hospital with Nubby in her arms, wrapped in a blanket. Two technicians were waiting.

"We've been called," one of them said. "Is he still breathing?"

"Yes," Lou said as she passed off Nubby to them. And just like that, Nubby was taken away.

Lou stood in the waiting room. She didn't know what to do.

An hour later, Mark came running through the doors of the hospital. Lou stood up and hugged him. She was so worried, but having Mark there helped calm her nerves. Just then, the veterinary technician walked into the room with the first update.

"We have him in an oxygen chamber in the intensive care unit," she said. "But he's having trouble."

They had given Nubby an X-ray and had found a defect in his esophagus, which is the tube that brings food from the throat to the stomach. There was a "pocket" that shouldn't have been there. When Nubby drank milk, some of it would get caught in that pocket instead of being swallowed. Then when he breathed, he would inhale the liquid, which would make him choke and spit up. There wasn't really any way to deal with this besides sitting him up each time he was fed. It was possible that the pocket would close up and heal itself as Nubby grew. But at this point, Nubby was still so small. And now he had lung problems. The veterinarians weren't even sure if he could survive long enough for them to find out whether or not the issue would heal on its own.

During visiting hours, Lou and Mark checked in on Nubby. He was sleeping, but they could see his tiny white head poking out of a tie-dye blanket that was wrapped around his body. There was a sign on the glass door of the oxygen chamber that said RESPIRATORY WATCH. There were sick dogs in the other kennels, too, which was sad to see. Sick dogs from all over the area were sent here. *Poor puppies*, Mark thought. *And poor Nubby*. He opened the little circular door—it was just big enough for a human hand to fit through—and touched Nubby's soft head. Nubby would spend the night here alone, but the staff at the hospital would be checking on him constantly.

"Call us if there is any change," Mark said.

Lou and Mark were trying to stay calm. They knew they had to take this one day at a time. Each day Nubby lived was a miracle. But if Nubby's esophagus didn't heal itself, he wouldn't have a great quality of life. And if he was living with a lot of pain, Lou and Mark would have to make a hard decision. There was a 50 percent chance that his esophagus would heal. But that meant there was also a 50 percent chance that it wouldn't. They couldn't help but worry.

# CHAPTER 5

## NUBBY'S MESSAGE

**EVER SINCE LOU HAD DECIDED** Nubby would be put in W.E.A.R.'s rescue program, Mark had been updating friends and family about Nubby on his personal Facebook account. And now that Nubby was in the veterinary hospital, a lot of people were cheering Nubby on and praying for him. It had been three long days since Nubby was first put in an oxygen chamber.

"Let's put Nubby on Facebook," Mark said. "Give him his own page." He wanted Nubby to have his own public Facebook page that anyone could follow, instead of sharing Nubby updates on his personal profile. Mark wouldn't mind writing the updates and taking photos and videos, even though it would take a lot of time—if Nubby had a special Facebook page, all the people who cared about him could get the latest news on his health right away. And maybe some would want to donate money for his rising hospital bills.

"I don't want to exploit Nubby like that," Lou said. "I am *not* on board."

There were other reasons why she didn't want to put Nubby on Facebook. She worried about whether or not Nubby would survive. Were they really going to introduce him to the world? What if he didn't make it? She didn't want other people to be sad, too. And she was nervous about what people would say. She didn't want to deal with online bullies. But friends and family kept urging her to put Nubby on social media.

"You have to be on board," a friend said. "Think of what Nubby can do for the rescue community. He can help other animals. You need to share Nubby with the world because he's an inspiration and he can help."

Lou knew her friends were right. Nubby was a warrior. Everyone at the animal hospital had fallen in love with the little two-legged pup, and plenty of people had started following Mark for Nubby updates. After all, she herself had already thought about how Nubby could teach others. Think of all the differently abled animals—and humans!—who could benefit from his story. The world needed Nubby.

It was settled. Nubby was getting his own Facebook page.

"I'm going to be upset if he gets more followers than me," Mark said just as he hit "publish" on Nubby's Facebook page. He wrote a post that introduced the world to the amazing dog with only two legs who was learning how to thrive despite the setbacks that were thrown his way. And he posted a few pictures of newborn Nubby, less than twenty-four hours old, as well as some photos showing Nubby's growth over the first month of his life.

Two hours later, Nubby had a thousand followers. Mark only had three hundred Facebook friends.

"Well, that little stinker!" Mark said.

By the end of the day, thousands of people had liked Nubby's page. Mark and Lou couldn't believe it!

The humans at the doctor's office had been very nice. Nubby could tell they loved him a lot. But he missed his Mom and Dad. Ever since Nubby had arrived at the vet, Mom and Dad were only allowed to see him once each day, then they had to leave. He didn't like being separated from them. And he missed his sisters, too. But today there'd been great news. He finally got to leave his little chamber and get in a truck, and now here he was back in his cozy living room with his soft, warm blanket and his other furry friends. Rita Rita, the little black one, was so happy to see him. Of all his new dog sisters, she seemed especially nice.

After five days in the hospital, Nubby was home. Mark and Lou were so relieved. But the veterinarians hadn't given him the "all clear." Mark didn't want to think about it, but no one really had any idea yet what Nubby's future would look like. Mark couldn't shake that feeling of uncertainty, but he didn't have time to dwell on it. He was too busy—Nubby's entire feeding pattern had to be changed. In the past, they'd fed Nubby with a bottle and then set him down. But now they knew that when they set him down horizontally on his bed, the liquid built up in his throat, and eventually caused him to choke.

To fix this, Mark and Lou had to feed Nubby while he was held upright in the crooks of their arms. This was not the proper way to feed a puppy. Followers on Facebook saw photos of Nubby eating like this and said, "You can't feed a dog that way!" But Lou and Mark continued on. It was best for Nubby—and it was what Nubby's doctors told them to do. Not only did they have to feed Nubby while he sat up, but then they had to keep Nubby propped up for twenty to thirty minutes after he ate. This allowed enough time for the liquid to drain down his throat.

Nubby still had to be fed often, but now

his feedings took much longer. Tonight, Mark would feed him while sitting in his computer chair in his office. It was late, and Mark was wearing pajamas. He propped Nubby up by holding the little puppy in his cupped hands on his lap. Nubby was so small that he still fit right into Mark's palms. Mark's head nodded forward. He was so tired. He wanted to sleep. But he needed to keep Nubby held upright. *By God, I'm not going to lose this dog*, he thought. Minutes later, Lou walked into the room and found both Mark and Nubby asleep in the computer chair. Mark was sitting up with his head dropped forward and his eyes closed. His glasses were sliding down his nose. Nubby's head was resting on Mark's cupped hands, still held upright. Lou snapped a photo. She wanted

Nubby's followers to know how much love Mark always gave to their rescues.

Nubby's Facebook page had taken off. People from all over the world started keeping up with Nubby's journey. Mark and Lou constantly shared updates, photos, and videos. The Dodo, a digital media company that tells stories about animals, had even written an article about Nubby's journey and his recent hospital scare. They included photos and videos from Nubby's new Facebook page. Donations for Nubby's veterinary bills started coming in, but more importantly, so did the messages. Lou and Mark weren't prepared for the effect Nubby had on the world. Every week, notes like this arrived in their inbox:

"We've seen you do it with Nubby so now we've taken a chance and adopted a blind dog!"

"We wait for you to post videos every week. Our daughter was born with no fingers and now she's five years old and can identify with Nubby. He never gives up on life!"

"I have cancer and look at pictures of Nubby while I do chemotherapy. If he can overcome his struggles and still be happy, then I can, too!"

Mark and Lou were overwhelmed. They'd had no idea how many families were out there dealing with challenges. They weren't alone—far from it! And through Nubby's story, families around the world could connect with and inspire one another. The message spread to people and animals across the globe: Different was not disposable! Nubby was helping people overcome challenges, helping them not feel sad anymore, and also helping other dogs get a second chance at life. There were abandoned pets out there who were now living great lives. And it was all because their owners saw Lou and Mark care for Nubby. It showed others that a dog with disabilities could live a great life.

"Nubby, you're a gift," Mark whispered as he softly petted the sleeping puppy.

# CHAPTER 6

## NUBBY ON THE MOVE

**NUBBY WAS FEELING GREAT. BITING** was so fun. And so was rolling. There was just one little thing: The other dogs got to run around and jump. When Nubby tried to do that, he fell over. Right now, all he could do was wiggle around. Maybe he'd learn how to walk one day when he was bigger like them. Until then, he enjoyed the special things he got to do. Like being pushed in a cart with wheels while Mom and Dad and his sisters took a walk. Sometimes Rita Rita joined him even though it was supposed to be his special carriage. She could be so bossy! He also got to rest in a carrier that Dad wore when he walked around. None of the other dogs got to do that. These things allowed Nubby to be taller than his dog sisters for the first time. He could see the tops of their heads and move almost as fast as they could! That was pretty cool. But right now he was thirsty and tired again. Playing was exhausting! Olivia Pig had taught him how to rest nicely on the couch. Maybe he should do that.

"I will just take a little snooze by my water bowl," Mark said as he narrated what Nubby was doing. "And then at midnight I will wake up the entire household because I will be ready to play."

It was mid-February and Nubby was five weeks old. He was napping—on his back as usual. The black four-leaf-clover-shaped splotch on his nose had become bolder and Nubby was looking especially cute. He was also getting some little spots behind his ears. His feet kicked a little. He must have been dreaming about running.

"Passed out wherever he's at," Lou said. "He doesn't care. BAM—taking a nap." Lou and Mark loved watching Nubby fall asleep in odd places. But he was doing a lot more than just sleeping these days. It was clear that

Nubby wanted to stand—and move! It started with his little doggy bed. It had a raised, rolled edge that would keep him safely inside. But he quickly learned how to pop out over the edge and get out. And it didn't stop there. When he was playing on the play mat in the corner of their living room, he'd rise on his hind limbs. He had gotten quite good at standing on his back legs, but then he'd eventually sway back and forth and fall over. It seemed like Nubby had finally figured out that he didn't have four legs. But it didn't seem to bother him.

Earlier that day, he had been playing on his LEGO "wheelchair." Using LEGOs, Mark had built a small platform with four truck wheels attached to it. He rested the front of Nubby's body on the platform and then secured him by wrapping a length of gauze around him and his wheels. Nubby could scoot himself across the floor by walking with his back legs. He had also learned how to army crawl around the house. He used his back legs to step forward, and the front of his body to wriggle straight ahead. His "nubs" were like elbows that he inched forward on a little bit at a time.

It seemed like nothing was going to stop this pup. And he kept growing! Despite his disability, Nubby was a full-sized boxer. That meant he was getting big fast—every day he gained a little bit more weight. This was great news, but it also meant that he was going to be a larger dog, and his heavy chest would be hard to support without front legs. A full-sized boxer could grow to be forty to seventy pounds. He wouldn't be able to use the LEGO "wheelchair" forever. Lou and Mark would have to figure out another solution soon. But at this point, he was growing too quickly for them to come up with a permanent fix.

Sometimes Mark wore Nubby in a baby carrier on the front of his body. And other times they pushed Nubby around in a doggy stroller. To keep his back legs strong, they would also use a sling or a "walking vest" that wrapped around the center of his body. It attached to a leash that Mark would hold to pull up Nubby's front end as he walked around their yard. They even put Nubby in a floaty in the pool so he could paddle with his back legs. It was good exercise. He wore a dog life vest of course! But as much as Lou and Mark wanted to pick him up and help him every day, they knew Nubby had to learn how to move on his own. And he had to keep exercising so he'd be strong enough to support himself as he grew.

Nubby's social media followers had questions: Would Nubby get a doggy wheelchair? Or prosthetic limbs, which were basically two human-made front legs? Was he seeing a special doctor or a physical therapist? Was he hurting himself by army crawling? When Nubby turned nine weeks old in mid-March, Lou and Mark decided to give everyone an update.

"Often the needs of large dogs like Nubby can't be addressed until they are almost six months old and their growth has slowed considerably," Lou told Nubby's followers. After all, Nubby was still about four months away from that! If they bought a doggy wheelchair now, he would outgrow it too quickly. It was better to wait until he was full-sized and then buy one wheelchair that would last him for years. "Although it seems we are taking too much time, we will have Nubby up and mobile long before many other dogs with a similar issue are up and mobile," Lou wrote. "We are humbly thankful for everyone's well wishes, thoughts, and following. We hope to continue to see everyone join his journey. In the face of all adversity he has been a shining light of hope for others born with disadvantages."

Sharing Nubby's story with the world had been amazing so far, but it was also causing some stress for Lou and Mark. They reminded themselves that Nubby's followers meant well when they gave advice, but that Nubby's doctors knew best. Together they'd figure out how to get this dog moving. Nubby already had a couple doctor's appointments set up to look at some options. Most likely, he'd be fitted for a set of wheels that lifted the front of his body and allowed him to roll his front forward by stepping with his back legs. But prosthetic limbs might be an option, too. Right now, his bones hadn't stopped growing yet. Maybe his "nub" and "nubby chicken wing" would grow a little longer. They'd have to wait and see.

Mark and Lou's goal was always to get their rescues healthy and adoptable. Nubby was on his way to reaching that goal even faster than they ever could have imagined! At his latest checkup, they'd gotten great news—Nubby's throat was healing on its own. As Nubby was growing, the pocket in his throat was growing smaller and smaller. It seemed like everything was going just as it should. Nubby was making progress all on his own, and that was more than they ever could have hoped for.

One spring afternoon in March, Lou noticed something unusual about Nubby's ears.

"Nubby, you started out with floppy ears this morning. Now they are standing straight up," Lou said. "What's going on, Nubby?"

Nubby stared at Lou with perked ears.

"His ears are bonkers," Lou said to Mark. "That's not normal for a boxer."

Uh-oh. Mark knew where this was going.

Lou was still worried that Nubby was deaf. But he did agree that Nubby's ears were wild. He could rotate his ears in different directions, which he had never seen a boxer do. "They're like satellite dishes," Mark said. "They got bigger. And bigger. And floppier."

Nubby's followers kept suggesting that Nubby was a mixed breed and that was why his ears were wonky. But Lou knew Nubby was 100 percent boxer! She had met his boxer parents the day she rescued Nubby. Even so, one ear was crooked, one was bigger than the other, and at one point they stood completely up for two days straight. Then they flopped back down.

"I was talking to someone who was very boxer knowledgeable and they said that deaf ears look like this," Lou said.

"Do you think he's deaf?" Mark asked.

He clapped near Nubby to see if he would move. He didn't.

For the next week, Lou and Mark made noises by Nubby to see if he could hear them.

"I think he might be deaf," Lou would say when Nubby didn't flinch after hearing a loud noise.

"He's absolutely not deaf," Mark would say when Nubby looked up as Lou's car pulled into the long driveway.

Finally, their question was answered: Nubby was sitting in the living room, his back facing Lou and Mark as the two of them stood in the kitchen. Mark opened a bag of potato chips. Nubby whipped his head around so fast you would have thought his favorite toy had just been tossed into the kitchen.

"That convinces me!" Lou said. "He's not deaf."

"He's just choosing to ignore us sometimes!" Mark said. "That little stinker."

# CHAPTER 7

## NUBBY TAKES FLIGHT

**NUBBY WAS NOW TWENTY POUNDS,** and he had transformed. He was bigger than Rita Rita! And in true Nubby form, he didn't let the fact that he had two legs slow him down. He had learned to hop. And jump. He was using his back legs to launch himself off the end of the bed, onto the couch, and across the floor. And he kept getting faster and faster at hopping. As the end of April neared and Nubby turned fourteen weeks old, Lou and Mark felt like a mini white kangaroo had moved into Hillcrest Manor.

*I can do it*, Nubby thought as he stared at the bed. This was his favorite challenge: jumping from the round pillow to the bench to the bed. It involved three soaring hops, and it ended with him flopping on the soft landing pad that was Mom and Dad's bed. *One, two, three!* Nubby felt the wind in his fur as he leapt into the air. Hop—hop—hop! He did it! Mom and Dad were laughing and cheering. They were covering the hard floor with soft mats and pillows so he could jump easier. His dog sisters liked it, too. They liked to play on the soft pillows with him, especially Rita Rita. She was funny. Nubby was glad he had met her. She was showing him how to play with toys. She taught him a game: You chew the toys in your mouth and then shake them until you can see the white stuffing come out. Whoever does that first wins.

"There is no holding him back," Lou said as she adjusted the pillow that sat on the floor near the end of her bed. Nubby liked to use that floor pillow as a launching pad. From there, he'd leap onto the low bench at the end of the bed and then soar onto the bed itself for a soft crash landing. His hops, jumps, cartwheels, and flops had become so daring that they had to let Nubby's followers know that Nubby was safe and sound—even during his acrobatics! After all, Nubby really didn't think he was different. This was just his special way of getting around. It was normal to him.

"There's really nothing that he can't do," Mark said.

"His tail is like a whip and he uses it like a pro!" Lou said. Lou had no idea that Nubby's tail could grow so long. But she was glad that it did because it was helping Nubby move better. Between his long tail and his long ears, he was quite a boxer. And to top it off, he had cute little spots on his rear end. "His front is boxer, but his back is spotty-butt kangaroo legs and tail."

Lou and Mark's house was starting to transform, too. Because Nubby liked to jump, they had to "Nubby-proof" their home the same way new parents "baby-proof" a house. When Nubby first started crawling, he would slip on the hardwood floors. And now that he had started to jump off the bed and the couch like a superhero, he really needed protection! He could jump two feet in a single leap. "He is a bona fide maniac on the couch and bed," Lou told Nubby's followers. They added round dog-bed pillows to the floor so he could hop from one pillow to another. And they covered as much of the floor as they could with rugs and play mats. Soon, it felt like their entire home was covered with area rugs, play mats, or pillows. Now Nubby could hop onto the bed or the couch with no help. But his preferred spot was sitting on the couch upright like a human, watching TV next to Mark.

They also made the gated area where he slept a little smaller so that his play space could be bigger. He and his sisters loved to roll around on the dog beds and play mats that were set up. Rita Rita especially liked to play-wrestle with him here.

Even though Nubby had become pretty mobile, he still needed help getting up or down the stairs. When Nubby was a puppy, it had been easy for Lou and Mark to carry him around. But he was growing like a weed—about half an inch every week. And he was a wiggly, active dog. Lou was only five feet two inches, so she had to start to rely on Mark (who was more than a foot taller) to carry Nubby up the stairs to the bedroom. He and the other dogs weren't supposed to sleep in Mom and Dad's bed, but Mark was so attached to Nubby, and Lou liked to sleep with Rita Rita. Rita Rita and Nubby had become quite the pair. Lou and Mark were always sharing photos and videos of the two playing together—and getting into trouble together.

Rita Rita knew that Nubby loved to chew just like she did. After a Saturday morning play-wrestling session with Nubby, she wanted to surprise him. She wanted to give him something even better than the brown monkey. Or the purple octopus. Or even the blue octopus! There was just one problem: She and Nubby were currently upstairs, and the surprise she was thinking of was downstairs. Rita Rita knew Nubby couldn't climb stairs on his own. She left Nubby to chew on Hedgie the hedgehog and sprinted down the steps. *Where are those shoes? Ah-ha! There's one.* She managed to get it in her mouth even though it was about the same size she was. She slowly dragged it up the set of stairs. *Nubby will love this!*

"Rita, did you bring that flip-flop to Nubs?" Lou asked. "I know he did not drag that size eleven Dad flip-flop up the stairs onto the play mat. And I'm not sure how your little butt did, either!"

"He has a conspirator!" Mark said. Nubby dropped the flip-flop from his mouth, but it was too late. There were already bite marks along the side of it. They couldn't believe the antics of Rita Rita and Nubby, and figured this wouldn't be the last time that Rita Rita brought Nubby a shoe. As if the two pups didn't have enough toys to keep themselves busy! Although, almost every toy Lou gave to Rita Rita and Nubby would end up falling apart within days.

"Did you kill that hedgehog?" Lou asked as Rita Rita and Nubby looked up at her innocently. The stuffed hedgehog was limp, and puffs of white stuffing were scattered across the floor. And that wasn't the only toy they had destroyed.

"So we have two squirrels injured, one monkey," Lou said as she gathered the remains of stuffed animals and placed them in a pile. "All these are in the hospital. We hold a funeral at 6:00 p.m. Rest in peace."

Lou and Mark laughed and laughed. Of course, they would have preferred that Nubby and Rita Rita didn't destroy every toy. But it made them happy to see Nubby play.

"Nubby sees the world like any other dog," Mark said. "He thinks he's just like the rest of the pack."

And that made them both very happy.

# CHAPTER 8

## CUSTOM NUBBY

"MARK, COME HERE!" LOU SAID. "Look at this comment on our Facebook page: 'All of us out here in Nubby Nation love you.' What the heck is Nubby Nation?"

It seemed that Nubby's followers had turned into one giant fan club, and they had nicknamed themselves "Nubby Nation."

"I like it," Mark said. "Let's turn it into a hashtag!"

Nubby Nation was growing, and there was no stopping it. This was shown by the mystery boxes that kept arriving at Lou and Mark's door. After Lou posted about Nubby's broken hedgehog stuffed animal, packages of new dog toys in all sizes, shapes, and colors were being sent to Hillcrest Manor. Nubby was getting more mail than Lou and Mark!

Nubby heard a noise at the front door. He chased Mom as she went to answer it. She grabbed a box. *Yes! Maybe it is another present!* Nubby sniffed the package. Lately, when Mom and Dad came in the front door, they brought boxes and envelopes with them. And they were usually fun things for Nubby. Each time, Nubby and his sisters got to lick and sniff the box while Mom or Dad opened it. *What will be inside today?* Mom pulled out something brown and fluffy. *Hedgie! A brand new Hedgie!* That was perfect because Mom said she couldn't perform surgery on the last hedgehog anymore. Whoever was sending these toys was very nice. Nubby would like to keep this toy for himself, but maybe he'd consider sharing it with Rita Rita. Maybe he could exchange the Hedgie for a Dad flip-flop. That seemed like a good trade. Rita Rita would like that.

"It may sound cheesy, but it is so appreciated and we are so thankful," Mark wrote to Nubby

Nation. "Thank you for doing such a little thing as sending a toy to 'everyone's' boy!"

For Nubby's fans, sending a toy was an easy way to show support. It made Nubby and his followers happy. But the rest of the things Nubby needed weren't so easily purchased at a pet store.

For example, many people wondered, "How does Nubby eat?" Since it was hard for him to lift the front of his body, a typical dog food bowl didn't work. Nubby's face would just fall into the bowl, which made it hard for him to chew and swallow. So Mark built Nubby a special stand. It was a small ramp that was topped with a silver dog food bowl. And it was perfectly Nubby-sized. Nubby could rest the front portion of his body on the ramp, which raised his head to the perfect height.

This way, he could chew and swallow in the proper position. It was like he was propped up on his elbows.

But as Nubby grew, so did his dog food bowl. At fifteen weeks, he was already on his third dog bowl contraption. It was lucky Mark was good at building things!

If Nubby were ever to get a wheelchair, or a "set of wheels" as Lou and Mark liked to say, those would have to be custom built, too. Nubby was one of a kind! He wasn't the first dog to be born with two legs—that was for sure. But most dogs who had been born with two legs didn't have partially grown legs like he did. Nubby had short bones where longer ones should have been. This prevented him from easily using a wheelchair device that other two-legged dogs might have used. Since Nubby wasn't flat chested like a typical two-legged dog, his wheels would have to be specially made. Getting lots of special sets of wheels made would be expensive, so Lou and Mark still planned on waiting until Nubby was fully grown before getting him fitted for a wheelchair. However, Nubby was getting big and he was very active. Would they really be able to wait until he was fully grown? This dog was not going to sit still—that much was clear!

In June, Nubby was five months old. The warm Texas summer was already in full swing. Nubby already had a favorite summer activity: jumping in the mist from the hose as Mark watered the garden.

Lou and Mark couldn't believe how quickly

the time was passing. They sure were staying busy! The month before, their first granddaughter, Lanie, was born. They knew she and Nubby would be great friends one day. And next month, when Nubby turned six months old, they would take him to the doctor to get his throat checked out one more time. It would be Nubby's final check just to make sure the pocket in his throat had healed correctly. They'd also examine his front limbs, his "nubs," to look at their growth. If his short front limbs grew long enough, they might be able to lengthen them with prosthetic limbs. That would help Nubby move like other dogs who had four legs. But right now his "nubs" were pretty short. They were long enough to interfere with a wheelchair, but not long enough for prosthetics to be attached to them. For now, his kangaroo-like hopping would have to do.

Mark walked through their big fenced-in backyard as the pack followed behind him. There was a wooded area the dogs loved to play in, but they also loved sniffing around the pond. In it were goldfish, minnows, and koi— some of whom were rescued. The koi were just another case where people had adopted an animal but then didn't know what to do with them once they got too big. *Then I guess those animals end up here*, Mark thought. He was more than happy to rescue an animal who needed saving. But he also wished that people who got pets realized they were committing to the care and growth of the pet for their entire life. Lou and Mark knew they couldn't rescue every animal. And they knew there weren't enough homes in Texas to house all the dogs who needed to be

**NUBBY** is a Boxer who was born without his front legs. Luckily, he was rescued by W.E.A.R. in Texas when he was just a few hours old.

Lou and her husband Mark had never taken care of such a young puppy before, but they stayed up around the clock to make sure Nubby was warm and had plenty to eat. They fed him with an eyedropper at first, and then with a bottle when he was a little older.

Nubby can't move like dogs with four legs, but that doesn't stop him! He loves playing with his dog sisters and lots of toys.

In fact, Nubby is always on the go! Lou and Mark make sure Nubby stays strong and healthy with plenty of exercise. Sometimes he rides with Mark in a sling. Other times he's in a sling on a leash so that he can use his back legs.

But Nubby has his own ideas about how to get around. Soon he's standing up on his back legs. Then he starts hopping! Nothing can stop him now.

HOP-

HOP-

HOP!
He did it—
go Nubby!

Nubby doesn't let anything stop him from living a happy life. And there are a lot of things that make him happy. Like playing with his sister Rita Rita.

Reading and snuggling with his human best friend, Laney.

And celebrating his birthday with his
family and pup-cakes that Lou baked!

Nubby has learned how to use a pair of wheels to get around—especially if it means he can say hi to kids or play with his sisters.

He even helps Lou and Mark take care
of puppies they're fostering, the way Rita
Rita and his sisters took care of him when
he was little.

Nubby brings so much joy and hope to Lou and Mark, and to the lives of everyone he meets. This special dog shows people every day that different is not disposable!

rescued. There were just too many of them. So they saved as many animals as they could, and focused on teaching people about how to help the others. It was the least they could do.

By now, Nubby had almost twenty thousand followers on Facebook. And his fans loved keeping up with the hopping two-legged wonder dog. But, of course, some people were concerned about Nubby. After all, he was getting to be quite a big dog, and all that hopping must have put some stress on his body. Lou and Mark had to send one more reminder to Nubby Nation.

"Nubby is in no more or less danger than any other average dog on an everyday basis. Of course, we take precautions with him and have modified things for his well-being. However, as much as possible, Nubby is treated and taught no different than any other four-legged dog. In other words, Nubby gets to be a dog like all the rest—a playful, learning, 'I can do it' dog. He just figures out how to adjust."

They felt better after sending that message. They wanted everyone to know how much Nubby was loved and that he was getting great care. Most people understood this! It was just a few people who were worried. The first time Nubby jumped it had scared Lou and Mark, too. But Nubby was perfectly safe. Lou looked at Nubby. He was playing with Mark in the living room. The two of them always had so much fun together.

Nubby was playing his favorite chase game. There were three dog beds set up in his play area. Dad would stand on one pillow and then step over to another. Nubby would follow Dad's path just one step behind him and hop from one pillow to another, too. Nubby tried to keep up with Dad's quick jumps. Hop-hop-hop! He fell, but he got right back up again. Oh, and part of the game was that he'd also bite Dad's toes! Today Dad was wearing red socks. They were especially good for biting. Dad moved to a new pillow. Nubby hopped, then fell again. But he got back up and managed to get a good bite of the red socks before Dad moved again.

"Ow!" Mark said. "That little stinker just chomped my toe!"

Lou shook her head and laughed. Mark would do anything for this dog—even if it hurt!

"No fear. No balance. No grace," Lou said. "But he's sure got some tumbling skills!"

# CHAPTER 9
## NUBBY'S FOREVER HOME

**RITA RITA AND NUBBY HAD BEEN** play-wrestling for an hour. Rita Rita was currently stealing a toy from Nubby, and then he'd chase her around the room until he got it back. It was yet another game they had invented. *Those two can entertain each other for hours,* Mark thought. He was watching the dogs from the computer chair in his office. But then something caught his eye—a message popped up on Nubby's Facebook page: "I am in New Jersey. I would be interested in adopting Nubby."

Thanks to Nubby Nation, Lou and Mark were getting messages like this from across the country. It seemed like every week there was another one. "When he becomes mobile and okay enough, will he be up for adoption?" A photo of a white boxer was accompanied by a silly message, "Hello from Gracie. I'm five years old and would love a little brother!" Another note simply said, "I would absolutely love to adopt him." The messages never stopped. Many people were interested in giving Nubby a home. *That's great news, right?* Mark thought. Then why didn't he feel better? Right now, it didn't matter how he felt. They couldn't adopt out Nubby until they were sure that he was 100 percent healthy.

But just as the adoption messages were coming in, so were a different kind of message. Some followers wanted to make sure Nubby never left Hillcrest Manor! Mark knew that most of Nubby Nation would be heartbroken if they did adopt out Nubby because then they wouldn't get daily updates on his life. But that was a lot of pressure on Mark, too! It was hard to see messages from Nubby's followers like:

"Will Nubby stay with you forever?"

"Please tell me you two will be his forever mom and dad!"

"May you be best buddies for many years!"

So far, the only response Lou and Mark

had given was different versions of the phrase, "We hope that's possible!" They hadn't committed to keeping Nubby. First, Lou and Mark had to seriously consider whether they could take on another pet. Being a pet owner was a serious commitment—whether it was a small goldfish or a giant horse. *Once you've made the commitment to care for an animal, you can't back down*, Mark thought. It requires a lot of patience, love, time, and kindness. As rescuers, they had to constantly remind themselves that they couldn't keep every animal who came through their home. Lou and Mark almost always thought, *I can't let this one go!* But they had to, especially if they wanted to keep rescuing other animals. They had to focus on the big picture: If they didn't give up this dog, how would they help the next one?

Even so, Lou always bawled her eyes out when they gave up a pet to their forever home. It never got easier.

Mark and Lou were doing all they could to raise money for Nubby to get him healthy, happy, and adoptable. They had held a yard sale and made Nubby-themed T-shirts to sell as a fundraiser, and Lou had taken on extra photography clients. Nubby's veterinary bills and possible wheelchair and prosthetics, and all the beds, toys, pillows, and food that he needed, were not cheap. But their philosophy had always been "Whatever it takes." They'd do whatever they needed to do in order to raise the money. But they'd both been working so hard with no breaks. And they still needed to care for Nubby's sisters, too. How long could they keep going at this pace?

From the beginning, Mark was very attached to Nubby. And Nubby adored Mark. The two of them could often be found cuddling on the couch together every night and watching TV, sometimes even falling asleep together.

"What are we going to do?" Mark asked as he petted Nubby. He knew Lou understood exactly what he was asking. They had had this conversation over and over again, but they hadn't come up with a final answer. Here were the facts: They already had four dogs. Keeping another one—especially a special dog like Nubby—was a huge undertaking. Lou reminded herself: *We can't possibly keep every dog we rescue.* She knew this. Mark knew this. Then why were they still having this conversation months later?

"Well, we have a lot of options," Lou reminded Mark. "A lot of people are willing to give him a forever home."

"I know we need to place the animals who come into the rescue. But I don't want him to leave," Mark said as he held Nubby tighter.

Lou looked at the two of them. Just as she couldn't imagine her life without Mark, she couldn't imagine their life without Nubby. A lot of animals had come through the doors of Hillcrest Manor. And they had found a home for all of them. But with Nubby it was just meant to be. He wasn't going anywhere.

"I guess he's becoming a part of the permanent pack," Lou said with a smile.

"You don't pick them; they pick you," Mark said as he squeezed Nubby. "Who are we kidding? He's going to stay."

Lou and Mark shared the news with the world. They posted on Nubby's Facebook page, and Nubby Nation went wild.

"I knew it! I knew it!"

"Congrats to your family!"

"Nubby Nation is not going away!"

Lou and Mark knew they had made the right decision. They didn't need their followers to tell them so.

# CHAPTER 10

## A STORM IS BREWING

**IT WAS A HOT JULY DAY AND MARK** was trying to measure Nubby. He was holding a long string. He wanted to wrap the string around Nubby's chest to see how many inches it was around. But Maggie kept getting in his way. She wanted to be measured, too! Mark wrapped the string around her chest just to make her happy. She was thrilled, and hopped joyfully away.

"Come here, Mr. Wiggle Spotty Butt," Lou said. Nubby, on the other hand, did not want to be measured. Between his jumping skills and the fact that he was now thirty-five pounds, it would not be easy to get this string wrapped around his body!

Mark and Lou had decided that even though Nubby was only seven months old and had not stopped growing yet, he needed some front mobility wheels. Front mobility wheels were two wheels that would support the front of his body. He didn't have two front legs to help him walk, but the wheels could help him move more easily while keeping his head propped up. Nubby would eventually need a second set of wheels and possibly even a third

set in the future since he hadn't stopped growing and the wheels couldn't be adjusted. It
wouldn't be cheap. But they had already started
saving up. The reality was that Nubby liked to
move! And they thought it was better to get
him used to wheels now while he was still a
puppy and he was willing to try something
new. If they waited too long, he might not even
want to try them.

With wheels, Nubby could actually go on a
walk with Lou, Mark, and the whole pack.
Right now, he had to sit in a stroller while the
rest of the dogs got to run. He wouldn't wear
the wheels all the time, but they would give
Nubby confidence and strength—and more
freedom! There were lots of companies that
made wheelchairs for dogs who didn't have
back legs, but there were only two companies

that made wheelchairs for dogs who didn't have front legs. Front wheels were more difficult to make, which made them more expensive. It was harder to find the right balance and measurements to make them roll smoothly. The first step was taking measurements. Then Lou and Mark could start talking to these two companies and see who could make Nubby the best set of wheels. They couldn't wait for the day Nubby would get to try them out for the first time.

It was raining. Hard. The August weather was dangerous and Hurricane Harvey was swirling above Houston. It was estimated that more than fifty inches of rain would fall—and fast. Lou and Mark were lucky. Even though it was raining at Hillcrest Manor, their property had not flooded. Other people had not been so lucky. People and animals were being evacuated—or leaving their homes—all over the area because water was flooding their homes and their yards. Some of the roads were completely underwater, so people were trapped in their homes and couldn't leave their neighborhoods unless they had a boat.

It broke Lou's and Mark's hearts. Lou cried just thinking about the people and animals who were struggling in the storm, the owners who had lost their pets, and the families who had escaped but desperately needed food and supplies until they could return home after the storm. She saw videos and photos on the news of cats and dogs swimming in the flooded roads, and pet owners putting their dogs and cats on floating inner tubes in an attempt to save their lives while they tried to escape the flood.

Lou wiped away her tears. She couldn't just sit and be sad about it. "Whatever it takes," she reminded herself. Instead, she and Mark sprang into action. And that's why their living room was currently full of even more animals than usual. There was a tiny black-and-white puppy named Windy Rain, a gray one-eyed Chihuahua named Blue, and a blue-and-gold macaw parrot named Coco.

Windy Rain had been found on a dirt road near a ditch during the storm. There were no homes or people nearby. She was probably only about six weeks old, she weighed less than two pounds, and she was covered in fleas. Lou and Mark spent the night warming her up. Her temperature was so low that they almost lost her. But she survived. And she was adorable. She reminded Lou and Mark of Nubby. He had been even smaller when he first arrived at Hillcrest Manor. It was hard to imagine since Nubby was now almost the biggest dog they owned! They'd easily be able to find Windy Rain a forever home once the storm passed, and she would grow to be big and strong with a family who loved her.

Blue was the pet of a fellow animal rescuer who'd had to evacuate because of the storm. Lou and Mark offered to keep Blue safe until she could return. While Blue didn't like Nubby, he loved Rita Rita, and she was happy to play with a dog her own size.

Coco the macaw's home was about to be flooded when Lou and Mark got the call to help. Her owner wasn't sure how to transport a bird during a storm. As the water was rising, Lou and Mark put Coco in a cargo carrier, then grabbed her five-foot-tall cage and loaded it into their truck. They made it to Hillcrest Manor safely, but within twenty-four hours, Coco's house was completely flooded with water up to the ceiling. Lou and Mark were so glad that Coco's owner had called them. They never wanted a pet owner to leave a pet behind during a storm like this. Pets needed to be evacuated, too, and Lou and Mark were more than willing to offer all the help they could give.

Seven dogs, one bird, and two humans. Hillcrest Manor was full, but Lou and Mark still felt like they weren't doing enough.

"It is devastating what is happening here. There are people who have literally lost everything. As a nonprofit, we strive to help people," Lou said. "We are safe, but we have to still extend our hand and try to do things for other people."

She and Mark were recording a video for W.E.A.R.'s and Nubby's Facebook pages to ask for help. Some of Nubby's followers didn't know that Nubby was rescued by W.E.A.R. And now W.E.A.R needed their help. Hopefully they'd be willing to give back, since Nubby had brought so much joy to their lives.

"That was how Nubby survived. Because we got a call. And now he's permanently here with us. We're fine, Nubby's fine, our pack is fine," she added. "But there are so many people who are not. When that happens, we need your support and we need you to be there with us."

Once Mark and Lou knew all the humans

in their area were safe and fed, they started focusing on the animals. The first step was to bring pet food to the pet owners who were evacuated, as well as the people who were stuck at home with their pets because all the nearby roads were flooded. Lou and Mark helped deliver food to these people by boat since they couldn't access a grocery store. Then they donated pet food to the local churches that were feeding evacuees. All the people who were affected by the storm were running out of pet food and were giving the little human food they had to their pets. If they had pet food, they wouldn't have to skimp on their own meals.

The next step was to start helping other animal rescues and shelters. At one nearby small rescue that had been hit badly by the storm, thirty dogs were in danger from the flooding, so the owners moved them to their living room to wait out the storm. Lou and Mark needed to deliver food, litter, beds, and blankets, as well as cleaning supplies to organizations like this and to others around Houston that needed it most. And that's why they were asking Nubby Nation for help. The donations started rolling in immediately.

"We appreciate everything y'all are doing," Mark said. "You all are wonderful. There are so many people who are helping here, it's amazing."

Lou nodded and hugged Rita Rita closely.

"It has to rekindle your faith in humanity," Mark said. "I know it has ours."

Nubby Nation came through. Within a few days, Nubby Nation had donated thousands of dollars as well as supplies directly to the organizations and people who needed it most. Lou and Mark's nonprofit had donated twelve thousand pounds of food and countless supplies across Texas. When the Category 4 hurricane had passed, it had caused $125 billion in damage. Lou and Mark knew it would take years for Texas to recover from this disaster. But with help from Nubby Nation, things were looking better.

"Texans will rise above," Lou said. And she meant it.

# CHAPTER 11

## NUBBY GETS ROLLING

**NUBBY WAS CURRENTLY BARKING** at Gracie. She was lying in Nubby's bed, and he was not happy about it.

"Nubby, you leave little Gracie alone!" Lou said. "She was lying there first. You gotta learn, Nubby. You gotta share."

Nubby was being a little stinker. Because of

Hurricane Harvey, all kinds of shipments had been delayed, but it was September now and Nubby's wheels had finally arrived. Lou and Mark had had a great stroke of luck: Someone from Nubby Nation also had a dog without front legs, and that dog, named Ruby Tuesday, had recently outgrown her set of wheels. Those wheels happened to be the perfect size for Nubby, so she donated them! Eventually, Nubby would outgrow these wheels and they'd need to place an order for a new set. But for now, the donated wheels would work just fine.

There was only one problem: Nubby hated them. He was so used to hopping that he didn't know how to roll. Even when the wheels were attached to his body he tried to hop. But that wasn't comfortable! And it wasn't how the wheels were designed to work. Rolling was a skill that he would have to learn—and it might take a long time.

"You're very stubborn, Nubby," Lou told him as she tried to get him to roll forward on their front lawn. "Other people have two-legged dogs who love their wheels, but our dog won't use them!" she said to Mark.

Nubby had always liked hopping, but now Mom and Dad had attached some kind of heavy thing to his body. It wasn't making hopping any easier. They kept trying to get him to move forward. They'd snap their fingers and wave their hands. They'd offer him toys and treats. But this thingy just seemed to slow him down. When would they take it off him? *Mom, Dad, I'm done now, thank you*

*very much*, he thought. *I'd like to hop on the grass now.*

Practice, practice, practice. That was all Lou and Mark could do for now. They reminded themselves that this was a scary and difficult transition for Nubby. But it would hopefully be worth it. His wheels would give him the ability to roll all around the yard outside and on walks, and they would help keep his back straight and strong.

Lou and Mark also had another plan in mind: They were going to talk to Derrick Campana of Animal Ortho Care in Virginia. He was known for making prosthetics for animals. He was one of the first people to ever do this. He had helped dogs of all sizes and abilities learn to walk. And he didn't stop there. He helped all kinds of other animals, too, from birds to horses to goats to elephants! Lou and Mark didn't know if prosthetics would work for Nubby. But they wanted to find out. His bones still weren't done growing. So they'd need to wait until he was more than a year old. It looked like Lou, Mark, and Nubby were all going to have to learn some patience!

Lou was standing outside in the backyard with Nubby. The leaves were changing color already, but it was warm for an October morning.

"Your form is looking great, Nubby!" she said.

It had been a month since Nubby first got his wheels, and he was getting much more comfortable with them. He could roll through the grass a few steps at a time. Lou couldn't wait to update Nubby Nation.

"Nubby does not know the meaning of 'hindered' or 'I can't,'" she wrote later that night. "We have hopefully given him the area, the means, and the resources to do anything he wants to just like any other dog. He has learned when to pull back, when he could harm himself, and when to just FLY and be all he can be!"

Nubby Nation loved to see the progress:

"You go, Nubby!"

"Thank you for saving him, giving him hope and love."

"We love you, Nubby! We'll wait as long as it takes you."

"He never ceases to amaze with all that he can accomplish!"

Now that Nubby had wheels and was officially a permanent part of the family, Lou had an idea. Part of W.E.A.R.'s mission was to visit schools and educate kids all about dogs and cats in need. Lou always said, "In order to change the future, we must teach the present." When she said that, she meant that problems couldn't be solved in the future unless you taught young people how to solve them today. Lou felt that, especially in Texas, there were far too many homeless dogs and cats. But there were so many ways to stop that from happening in the first place! And that's what she wanted to talk to the kids about.

Thanks to Nubby, now she had a second subject to teach. She had always felt that

Nubby could send a great message to the world. And that was, "Different is not disposable," which meant that differently abled animals could make great pets, too. The popularity of Nubby's Facebook page had proved that she was right! Kids of all abilities would embrace Nubby, too. She knew it. It was settled: Nubby was going to go on his first school visit.

"Busy day today," Lou posted on Nubby's Facebook page. "We will be teaching and visiting with a school in Houston. Wish him luck and send good thoughts. He can do it!"

Nubby's first official school visit was in December. It was Lou's last school visit of the year. After this visit, W.E.A.R. would have taught more than sixteen hundred public school students about dogs and cats in need. A session with Nubby was the perfect way to end 2017.

Lou ran around the house packing everything Nubby needed. He had just had a bath so he was nice and clean. She packed his food, water bowl, and harness in a bag, then loaded Nubby's favorite stroller into the truck as well, just in case he didn't like using his wheels. She carried Nubby to the truck, then buckled him into a doggy car seat, which is basically a basket that secures to the seat. The school wasn't too far away, so their drive was short. As she unloaded Nubby and his gear in the school parking lot, she hoped that Nubby would behave well in front of the kids. This was a big day for W.E.A.R., and for Nubby, too.

Nubby had never seen so many tiny humans before. And they all wanted to pet him! And, oh boy, did he want to be petted by them! He moved forward as quickly as he could into the crowd of kids. *Oh, hey, that's how these things work*, he thought. *These wheels are actually okay sometimes*, Nubby realized. But right now he didn't care much about the wheels. He just wanted to see these kids! *Hello! Hello! Oh, hey! And hello to you, too! Ooh, you smell like cookies!*

When Nubby was surrounded by kids at the school, he began rolling without a problem. It was as if he forgot he was wearing his wheels. He wanted to greet each child in the room and they were the fastest way to do it.

"Look! He's using his wheels!" The kids said as they crowded around Nubby. "Come on, Nubby!"

Lou was so proud of Nubby. He lit up when he saw the kids. She knew that Nubby was helping these kids learn compassion, which means that you care about others—especially those in need—and are willing to help them.

"He's still a dog, but he's different," Lou said. "Can pets be different?"

"Yes!" The class said.

Nubby beamed. It looked like Nubby had earned a permanent position as ambassador for W.E.A.R.

# CHAPTER 12

## NUBBY TURNS ONE

**NOW THAT NUBBY HAD WHEELS,** Lou and Mark had to make more changes to their home. They didn't want Nubby to feel left out or different. Mark had originally built their home. And although Hillcrest Manor looked like a typical two-story home from the outside, it was different on the inside. When you walked through the front door, it looked more like a garage workspace. This first floor was where they kept a lot of supplies for their animal rescue organization. Up the stairs was a second-story apartment where they lived with, a kitchen, living room, and bedroom.

Not only did Nubby need more space to play, but he was also far too big for Lou to be carrying him up and down the stairs every day. So it had been settled. They were renovating their house to make it more like a traditional home, with a kitchen and living room and bedroom downstairs. And, of course, plenty of room for Nubby. Maybe one day they could add on an addition especially for the rescue organization. It could have more storage and a place to wash and care for the dogs they rescued. Mark had a lot of ideas, but it was a big enough undertaking already. He was doing all the work on his own, but he was making progress. Nubby's "condo" was the first priority.

"We didn't realize what it was going to take at the time," Mark said to Lou as he held open the new half door to Nubby's "condo." Lou agreed. They were sure some people thought that renovating a home for a dog was silly, but Nubby really did need a new, safe space. After all, they couldn't keep Nubby in a doggy daycare if they ever left for a few hours, because Nubby had special needs and other people didn't know how to care for him. But if they let him loose in their house, he'd chew everything. So they built Nubby a special, safe room of his own under the stairs complete with a light and a half door where he could be left alone occasionally for short periods of time. It had soft pillows on the floor as well as his favorite toys. They even hung up framed photos of Nubby, his family, and other animals W.E.A.R. had rescued. Underneath was a shelf to store his toys and display more framed photos. The finishing touch was a bronze plaque. It had been sent to Nubby by a fan from Ireland. It had two hands holding a heart with a crown on top. It was an Irish symbol that represented friendship, love, and loyalty. It was perfect.

By the time Nubby's first birthday rolled around on January 9, his condo was complete. Nubby sat on a round pillow. He wore a blue shirt that said "Birthday Boy" and a red hat that said "Happy Birthday." Maggie wore a spotted tutu. Rita Rita wore a navy-blue polka-dotted dress. Lou and Mark took turns opening presents that Nubby Nation had sent and reading the cards out loud to Nubby.

"Dear Nubby and family. Have a very happy first birthday. Thank you for all you're doing to educate people. Enjoy your presents and share with Rita Rita and your other sisters."

"Happy first birthday, Nubby! Sending love from California."

"Nubby, you have made us better people. You are a warrior."

Mark and Lou shared a live video of the party, and it was watched more than twelve thousand times. There were nine hundred comments on the video from all over the world: Austria, Spain, Brazil, Taiwan, Mexico, the United Kingdom, Australia, the Netherlands.

And they all wanted to wish Nubby a happy birthday.

"Nubby, look! A new hedgehog. And new squirrels!" Lou said as she handed Nubby some of his gifts. He immediately started biting them and shaking them around like Rita Rita had taught him.

"Are you ready for cake, Nubby?" Mark asked. Lou grabbed the muffins—one for each dog.

"Happy birthday to Nubby . . ." they began to sing. "Hey, sit down, Maggie!"

Holding birthday muffins in front of three dogs and making them wait through an entire birthday song was impossible. Lou set down the muffins and let them dig in. It was a good thing they hadn't invited Olivia Pig and Gracie to the party. It would have been too much chaos. And they weren't big partiers, anyway.

"What do you think, Nubs?" Mark asked.

"That muffin is too big for Rita!" Lou said.

"Small bites, Nubby," Mark said as he broke off a piece for Nubby. "I think he's going to eat the whole thing."

Lou laughed.

"They think this is pretty darn delicious," Mark added as all three dogs took more bites.

Nubby licked his lips and balanced on his back two legs so his head was held high. Were there any more muffins? Mom called them "pup-cakes." And she had let Maggie lick the beaters when she was baking this morning. Nubby was happy he had waited for the finished muffin. And boy, oh boy, look at all these new toys. He and Rita Rita were going to have a blast! Nubby was happy to share his birthday toys with his sisters. They had taken such good care of him the past year. It was the least he could do. That's why he didn't mind that Rita Rita had just eaten the last muffin. She deserved it.

Lou decided to speak to the camera for all the people who were tuning in to watch the video live.

"For a dog who truly beat all the odds, Nubby turns one year old today," she started. "One year ago, our phone rang here at W.E.A.R. about a dog who was born with no front legs. He put us through the ringer, but look at him now. You have been his village, his family. He is your dog, too," Lou added.

"You've all given us a lot of hope when we were having our tough days, and we so appreciate that," Mark said. "All of you just believing in him. We know that we believed in him but it's still a hard road some days."

"Nubby is teaching people it's okay to be different," Lou added. "It can be scary, but it's okay."

"From us to y'all: Happy birthday, Nubby!" they said. "We declare the rest of the week a celebration!"

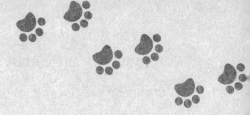

# CHAPTER 13

## NUBBY ON THE ROAD

**SUMMER HAD BEEN BUSY! LOU AND** Mark couldn't believe it was already July. They had spent most of the spring preparing for this day: the start of a big road trip from Texas to Virginia to see Derrick Campana at Animal Ortho Care.

Derrick couldn't promise anything for

sure, but at least Nubby had an appointment. Derrick would take a cast of Nubby's chest, then get to work on coming up with some kind of solution to help Nubby move more easily. Lou hoped that Nubby would be more cooperative than he was when they measured him for his wheelchair. It had taken three people to keep Nubby still and get the exact measurements last time! If only she could explain to Nubby exactly what was going on. She wondered if he'd be more willing to sit still if he understood—or less! After all, he was a happy camper just as he was.

Nubby Nation was especially excited and had donated more than a thousand dollars to get Nubby to Virginia. Everyone wished the best for Nubby and was so excited to see what Derrick might be able to do. Mark and Lou had rented a minivan, folded down the back seats, and covered it with tons of blankets. Lou and Mark would take turns driving while Nubby, Olivia Pig, and Rita Rita rode in the back.

Their trip would be long—from Texas to Arkansas to Tennessee to Virginia—and they had promised they'd share their route so Nubby's followers could come and meet them along the way. They hesitantly posted which rest stop they were pulling over to first. They didn't really expect people to show up, but as they pulled in they saw a crowd. It was Nubby Nation! It turns out that Nubby's fans were desperate to meet him in person. And Olivia Pig and Rita Rita, too. Lou and Mark were shocked.

Nubby loved road trips! He got to sit in the back of a van with lots of soft blankets. It was fun! Olivia Pig and Rita Rita were cuddling with him, too. Sometimes it would get boring, but then it would get fun again when they'd stop somewhere and get out of the car. At each stop, there were friends waiting for them. They would pet Nubby and take pictures of him. If road tripping meant meeting lots of friends, then Nubby was all about that life!

Lou and Mark continued to be amazed at every stop they made. They met Nubby's followers at local dog parks and rest stops. At one park, thirty people were cheering and holding up signs as they pulled in. Lou and Mark wore matching T-shirts that said, "Road Trippin With Nubby," so people could more easily find them. But spotting a hopping two-legged boxer was pretty easy!

As they got closer to Virginia and met more of Nubby's followers, their hope for the appointment with Derrick grew. They didn't want to let Nubby or his fans down. That was never fun. In May, they had gotten Nubby's third set of wheels. These wheels were more lightweight. And even though Nubby had gotten better at using his wheels, and he liked this set of wheels more than the last two, he still didn't love wheel life. At that time, they had to update Nubby's followers:

"Nubby has not showed us he is scared or uncomfortable when he is in the wheels.

However, he would prefer to just sit and look and wag when he is wearing them. No amount of food, treats, joyful play, toys, or 'chase the pack' prompting has fueled his desire to run carefree in his wheels chasing butterflies and squirrels. He is one stubborn boy. I do think Nubby was put on this earth to teach us patience, time, and commitment."

Even though Lou and Mark knew so much about dogs, this was one problem they couldn't solve on their own. They reached out to a dog behavior expert to try to help them understand what else they could do to get Nubby excited about his wheels. At the very least, Nubby had to use his wheels to keep his spine and back healthy and strong.

And that's why this appointment with Derrick meant so much. They would be so happy to find a different way that Nubby could move around. They had warned Nubby Nation, though. They didn't want to promise anything.

"There is ZERO guarantee on how Animal Ortho Care can help Nubby. But we do feel they are the best team to come up with an out-of-the-box idea. We are fully aware Nubs might not have enough limb to do an actual prosthesis, but we will never know if we do not GO!"

And that was their mindset going into it: *We'll see how it goes. You never know unless you try!* They'd always trusted Nubby's doctors, and they would only try something if it made a positive change for Nubby.

Lou, Mark, and Nubby stepped into Derrick's office for their casting appointment. Lou admired the framed photographs surrounding the patient table. In each frame was a different animal with a unique kind of prosthesis or brace. Each one had had a different situation, and Derrick had figured out a creative way to help them walk. Hopefully he'd be able to come up with something just as creative for Nubby. But for now, they'd just have to wait and see.

"Nice to meet you, Nubby!" Derrick said. He was wearing a red T-shirt and a smile that sparkled through his scruffy mustache and beard. Lou and Mark were happy to finally meet him in person. He got to work right away by laying Nubby down on a floor mat and inspecting his "nubs."

Nubby was in a room now. They had stopped driving and he got to meet another nice human. This one was named Derrick. Nubby could smell another dog on Derrick, which meant he had a pet dog at home. That was good. Derrick inspected Nubby's body. That part was a little strange. And Rita Rita wouldn't stop sniffing Nubby while it was happening. She wanted to oversee the appointment and make sure everything was okay.

Then Derrick made Nubby sit up, and it looked like he wanted to wrap something around Nubby's body. Nubby didn't want to be wrapped up! Could he go back in the car now? He had gotten to pee in four different states so far, and that was way more fun than this doctor appointment!

When it was time for Derrick to create a cast of Nubby's body, Nubby didn't want to cooperate. Derrick needed to wrap cloth around his body, wait five minutes for it to dry, then cut it off. The cast of Nubby's body would help him try out ideas and potentially build some kind of walking device for Nubby. As he wrapped Nubby, Mark tried to hold him still. Once the cloth was tightly wound around his body, Nubby was more calm.

"Good boy, Nubby," Mark said as he gave Nubby a kiss.

*Maybe Nubby realized that this is important to me and Lou*, Mark thought. In the backs of their minds, they still really hoped Derrick could do something. If not now, then in the future. It wasn't just about helping Nubby. It was about helping all dogs who were born without front legs. Because a solution for Nubby could be a solution that helped thousands of other pets.

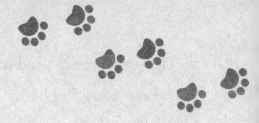

# CHAPTER 14

## A ROADBLOCK
## FOR NUBBY

**IT HAD BEEN ONLY THREE WEEKS** since the road trip. After traveling more than three thousand miles, everyone at Hillcrest Manor needed a break! Nubby had been particularly sleepy on this August afternoon.

"What's wrong with Nubby?" Lou asked.

"This is his playtime usually," Mark said.

"He's been really tired today. I'm worried."

Lou agreed. Nubby was not acting like himself. He was lying on a mattress in his play area. Nubby was usually so rambunctious that they'd had to add this extra-soft mattress outside Nubby's condo. The padded play mats weren't cutting it. He was only getting larger, heavier, and more active! But today he wasn't rolling around and jumping on the mattress. He was falling asleep on it.

"It's getting later in the evening and it's been a rough day," Mark said. "This is where we are going to sleep tonight," he said to Lou as he pulled a pillow onto the mattress right next to Nubby. He didn't want to let Nubby out of his sight.

The next day, Nubby was still not himself. And he was looking thin. Usually Lou and Mark fed Nubby a very special diet so he stayed a healthy weight. He ate just the right amount of food two to three times a day. Because he didn't have two legs to support the front of his body, his weight was very important. He couldn't get too heavy or it could hurt his hips or back. But they also didn't want Nubby to be too thin. So it was easy for Lou to tell when Nubby had lost just one pound. And he had just thrown up his dinner.

*He's sick*, Lou said to herself. Mark had left earlier that day for Austin for a work trip. *Something's not right*. Lou stayed close to Nubby. But her worst fears came true. Nubby continued to throw up during the night. *This is not a good sign*.

Rita Rita was watching Nubby from across the room. She was worried. Her best friend was so sick. Rita Rita used to be bigger than Nubby. Now Nubby was much bigger than her. But she still wanted to care for him. She had tried bringing Nubby some toys, but he didn't want to play with any of them. He had just looked tired and sad. She hoped Mom could make Nubby feel better, and fast.

Bright and early the next morning, Lou put Nubby in her car. She called the veterinarian as she drove toward his office. "He's lethargic and sleeping a lot," she explained. She started having flashbacks of the last time she rushed Nubby to the veterinarian. That time had been terrifying. Hopefully this time wouldn't be as scary.

When Lou arrived, the vet took Nubby's blood work and did an ultrasound immediately. The news wasn't good: Nubby was not healthy. But they weren't sure exactly what was happening yet. Lou started to panic.

"What else could go wrong?" Lou said to Mark over the phone. Mark decided to rush home to be with Nubby and Lou.

Lou posted to Nubby's Facebook page: "Nubby needs prayers. I need prayers and his Daddy who is in Austin rushing home needs prayers. Will keep everyone informed as soon as we know something."

The veterinarians got to work. They gave Nubby shots, antibiotics, and fluids. They put him back in the oxygen chamber. It was very important that he ate a little bit of food that night and did not throw it up. If he threw up in the next twenty-four hours, they'd have to do surgery to see what was wrong.

Lou was feeling especially sad. *What else could go wrong?* She couldn't stop repeating that phrase to herself. But then it hit her: She couldn't live her life every day thinking that she or someone she loved might get sick or injured. *Live your life with joy and hope*, she told herself. *Joy and hope.*

The next morning, Nubby's temperature had returned to normal. He hadn't thrown up the dinner he'd eaten late last night. That was great news. But he was still very sick. He still was weak. He still was not moving around much.

And he was continuing to lose weight. He'd dropped four and a half pounds in one week.

"He looks like a little skeleton," Mark said when they visited Nubby a few days later. After a lot of tests, the veterinarian had finally figured out what was wrong with Nubby: He had suffered from full-blown pancreatitis and the beginning of liver failure. Unfortunately, Nubby was still having issues on his insides. You couldn't see those issues from the outside, but they were there. Luckily, the vet had some ideas on how to make Nubby feel better and prevent him from getting sick again.

Whew! Nubby felt awful. His insides had hurt so much, but then the nice humans had taken care of him. They were the same humans who weighed him and gave him shots and X-rays sometimes.

This week they gave him a lot of medicine, and now he was feeling much better. And Mom and Dad and Rita Rita had visited him every day. Nubby remembered being here before when he was younger. Back then, he was scared that he wouldn't be able to come home again. But he knew now that he'd be able to go home soon. They were just making sure he was feeling better. He'd make sure to let them know that he was ready to go home today.

After just a few days, Nubby's ears were perking up. That was a good sign! He even tried to play with Rita Rita when she visited him at the hospital. He got tired very quickly, but that was okay. He ate his food, and he even went to the bathroom. These were all great signs! The veterinarian said Nubby could go home tonight. He'd need a lot of time to rest and recover, but he *would* be okay. Nubby would now have to be on an even more special diet. After learning that Nubby had a very sensitive stomach, the vet wanted Nubby to only eat a very limited amount of ingredients in his food. And treats had to be truly just treats—he couldn't have them often. As long as they followed that diet, Nubby should be fine.

"Once again, in Nubby fashion he bounces right back," Mark said. It truly felt like another miracle. Nubby Nation agreed.

"He had us scared!"

"Thank heavens that Nubby is getting better!"

"Glad you're feeling better now, Nubby! Sending a massive hug from England."

"Nubby has so many fans! We are all so happy he is doing much better."

The messages made Lou smile. Nubby Nation really did have their backs. *Joy and hope*, Lou reminded herself. *Joy and hope*.

# CHAPTER 15

## NUBBY GETS BIG

**AT 1:33 IN THE MORNING LOU WAS**
still awake. Both Nubby and Rita Rita were
in her bed and they were not making it easy for
her to fall asleep.

"Nubby, if you could quit farting on my
shoulder that would be great. And Rita Rita,
kindly get your paw out of my eye."

Being a mom to five dogs was no joke. Especially now that Nubby was the biggest dog they owned. Nubby weighed in at forty-four pounds. When he stood on his hind legs, he was almost as tall as Lou. And today, on January 9, 2019, Nubby was two years old.

"Mark doesn't get a birthday party anymore—just Nubby!" Lou told Nubby Nation that day. Nubby's second birthday had all the usual guests: Maggie, Rita Rita, Mark, and Lou. But there was one additional guest: Lanie! Mark and Lou's granddaughter had become great friends with Nubby just as Lou had expected. They played with each other's toys and took naps together, and Nubby even let Lanie touch his nubs. He pulled away when anyone else tried to touch his front limbs. But not Lanie. Lanie loved Nubby so much that she gave Nubby her pacifier once. He ate it. Lou and Mark didn't know until he pooped out a pacifier in one piece.

"Don't share your pacifier with the dog!" They'd have to teach Lanie the difference between dog toys and human toys!

Mark continued to unwrap Nubby's presents while Lanie held the birthday cards. She wasn't even two years old yet, but she loved to help out, especially for her friend Nubby. Her brown curly hair bounced around her sweet face as she watched Nubby play happily with his new toys. Nubby got another new Hedgie, a blue dragon, a red squeaking chameleon, and a gray triceratops.

Then it was time for pup-cakes! But as soon as Lou brought over the muffins, chaos broke out. Maggie ate Lanie's muffin! Then Nubby ate two muffins at once. Lou sat down with a new muffin for Lanie and Mark and they quickly took bites before the dogs could see. Lou looked around the room at her family as they began to sing happy birthday to Nubby. The room was full of chaos—and love—and she knew that people all over the world were celebrating Nubby, too. She could feel the support and well wishes surrounding them and it made her smile.

"I can't believe we made it this far," Mark said. Lou agreed.

Nubby's birthday had been a ton of fun. But it was time for Lou and Mark to update Nubby Nation about something that had been on their minds. Everyone—including Mark and Lou—had been so excited about their trip to Virginia to see Derrick. But that had been almost six months ago. Nubby's followers wanted to know: Was Derrick going to do anything for Nubby? Couldn't he make prosthetic front legs for Nubby like he had done for so many other animals?

"This is his update," Lou said to the camera. She was recording a live video for Nubby's Facebook page, and almost three thousand people were watching. She was sitting cross-legged on a floor pillow with Rita Rita in her lap. Nubby was jumping around in front of the camera playing with some of his stuffed toys. "The bottom line is, it's not going to happen. Nubby does not have enough skeletal length on his front paws to do what so many have said might happen. Prosthetics are not going to work for Nubby."

Lou didn't like sharing bad news with Nubby Nation. But sometimes things didn't turn out like you hoped for. Nubby had two nubs, but they weren't long enough to attach prosthetic legs to. There was also another issue: They had visited Derrick in July, and when Nubby had gotten sick in August he had lost a lot of weight. That meant the cast that Derrick had taken of Nubby's body wasn't correct anymore.

Even though Nubby had recovered from being sick very quickly, he had gotten much skinnier and had dropped down to less than thirty-five pounds. That was too skinny. Lou and Mark worked hard to get him back up to a healthy weight, even though his diet was now limited. It took almost three months to get him back to forty-six pounds. They still needed him to gain two or three more pounds and then maintain that weight. Nubby was active and young, so he burned a lot of calories. It was hard to keep weight on him! Once Nubby was back to his regular weight, Derrick could continue to think about how Nubby's body cast could be used in a more creative way to help him learn how to walk more easily.

"It was not a wasted trip," Lou reminded Nubby's fans. She scratched Rita Rita's head as Nubby continued to play with a blue dinosaur toy. "They are still working with us. Instead, we are looking at more innovative ideas. It's a long process. And we don't have the answers yet. We have suffered a lot of stuff getting him to two years, but he is one healthy pup now and he should live a long and healthy life."

Lou and Mark had made some adjustments

to his wheelchair, and Nubby was starting to use the wheels better. When he was outside, he did exercise and therapy with his wheels on. He also went for walks outside with them on. When he was inside, he got around by hopping and jumping on soft pads around the house. This was Nubby's way of life, and he was doing great so far.

"Nubby is teaching the world and paving the way for other animals with disabilities," Lou added. "Rest assured, he's happy, he's healthy, and he has a lot of love. Nubby, say bye!" Lou shut off the camera. She hoped Nubby Nation would understand. Many people had seen three-legged dogs or two-legged dogs who used prosthetic legs with ease. But Nubby was different. Lou and Mark hoped that every-one understood they were doing all they could for Nubby. They wanted him to walk more easily just like everyone else did.

There were more than a hundred comments on the video, and they made Lou and Mark feel better:

"You both do an amazing job. Nubby is where he needs to be. Love to you all!"

"Hi, spotty Nubby! So glad you're healthy and back to a good weight. Keep up the good work!"

"Don't listen to the negative comments. I know you are doing the best for him!"

"He is always happy and you guys are AWESOME for saving him!"

"You're the best parents Nubby ever could have gotten!"

Lou and Mark were glad to have Nubby Nation on their side, and they were happy to get that conversation over with. Now they could focus on some good news that they hoped to share soon: Nubby was getting a video! The Dodo, the company that had written an article about Nubby when he was just five weeks old, wanted to make a longer video about his life. They had been following Nubby's journey on social media and thought he had an amazing story to tell.

They had sent a camera crew to Hillcrest Manor. It had been two exhausting days of filming, but Lou and Mark were so proud of Nubby. Usually when Mark whipped out his camera to record something, Nubby would stop whatever funny thing he had just been doing and stare at the camera. He had been so afraid Nubby would stop and stare when the professional film crew arrived. But he didn't!

And neither did Lanie, even though she was the same age as Nubby—just two years old. They couldn't wait to see what The Dodo did with all the footage they had recorded, and how the world would react to Nubby's story.

Nubby's video aired in March. It was part of a series called *Comeback Kids* and it was called "Nubby the 2-Legged Boxer Steals His Dad's Heart." Lou and Mark couldn't wait to share it with Nubby Nation. And they were so excited for the rest of the world to meet Nubby, the dog who had brought so much joy and inspiration to their lives. More than thirty-seven million people watched it and forty-two thousand people left comments. Nubby's story had been viewed by more people than Lou and

Mark ever could have imagined. Nubby Nation kept growing!

"I just saw the video and fell in love with Nubby!"

"You are a star, Nubby!"

"Nubby, you are wonderful just like your parents!"

"I laughed and I cried. Bless you both for helping Nubby and the other dogs."

"You have new fans in Nebraska, Nubby!"

"I need your autograph, Nubby!"

And just like after the first time they shared Nubby's journey with the world, Lou and Mark saw so many amazing stories pour in. People posted photos of their differently abled dogs in the comments. Dogs with two legs. Dogs with three legs. Dogs who couldn't use their back legs. Dogs who used wheelchairs and dogs who didn't. Dogs who hopped around just like Nubby. There was even a gray striped cat named Nubby who was born without her front legs as well!

Nubby Nation now had more than fifty thousand followers. In July, Lou and Mark had one more request: a fourth wheelchair for Nubby. Nubby had grown four inches longer over the past year, which meant his previous set of wheels no longer fit. This was exactly what they had been worried about in the beginning—that they'd have to order multiple sets of wheels. But at the same time, they knew it was what was right for Nubby. And thanks to the kindness of others, they'd been able to make it happen for Nubby each time.

"Fingers crossed for the last set. What do y'all think? Nubby needs new wheels! Can y'all help one more time?" Lou and Mark posted to Nubby's Facebook page. "Nubby is hopefully at his full size and height. His growth has stopped. If you would like to contribute please donate to W.E.A.R. for 'Nubby Wheels.' We thank you all!"

Four days later, they were able to place an order for Nubby's new wheels. Lou cried and cried. She was overwhelmed by the kindness of Nubby Nation. Nubby really did belong to all of them. He was everyone's boy. All fifty thousand of them.

# CHAPTER 16

## NUBBY'S PUPPIES

**LOU, MARK, OLIVIA, RITA RITA,** Nubby, and Lanie had just left on a road trip. They were supposed to head to Galveston, Texas, for a mini beach vacation. But before they got there, they had already turned around to head back home to Houston. When they left the house, they had three dogs in their truck. Now they were driving home with seven.

While they were headed toward Galveston, Lou had gotten a call from a friend of a friend. An older woman's eight-year-old pet Chihuahua had unexpectedly given birth to four puppies—and two of those puppies had only two legs. The pet owner was disabled and couldn't drive the puppies to the vet. And she couldn't afford five dogs. She needed someone else to care for these puppies. Plus, the mama dog's milk had dried up and the puppies hadn't eaten in twenty-four hours. Someone had to save these puppies—fast.

"Our job is to take care of these animals," Lou said. "We have to help so that this doesn't happen again."

Mark agreed, and turned the truck around.

Their vacation could wait. Not only was W.E.A.R. going to rescue the puppies, but Lou was going to make sure the mama Chihuahua was spayed so that she wouldn't have any more babies. This would be good for the pet owner, good for the pet, and good for all dogs out there. There were already so many dogs in Texas—and around the country—who needed homes. Lou and W.E.A.R. would make sure these four puppies found forever homes. *One dog at a time*, she reminded herself.

The "little pack" had arrived. Even though Hillcrest Manor was full of dogs, Lou and Mark still took in rescue animals for W.E.A.R. whenever they could. And the four puppies they had picked up on the way to Galveston, Sweet Girl, Mo, Jules, and Dinky, were temporarily living at Hillcrest Manor. They were tiny brown and white Chihuahua puppies who were born in mid-July. They were now four weeks old. Two of the pups, Mo and Jules, were doing especially well. The other two, Dinky and Sweet Girl, were much slower to make progress. That's because Dinky and Sweet Girl each had only two legs. Just like Nubby. And they weighed less than one pound each.

"Our village, we know, is strong. Together we can make a difference in their little lives," Lou wrote on the W.E.A.R Facebook page. "Stay on this journey with us, donate to help if you can." Lou hoped to raise more than a thousand dollars to help all four puppies get properly cared for by a vet and get microchipped.

The "two-leggers," as Lou liked to call them, weren't eating well. And they weren't going to the bathroom regularly. Lou and Mark were a wreck. It reminded them of their first few days with Nubby. These pups were a few weeks old, which was great, but they needed those two to catch up to their four-legged siblings. The smallest one weighed only eight ounces. Mark and Lou were up again around the clock bottle-feeding the smaller two puppies. The larger ones had moved on to puppy food. The pups with two legs needed to be propped up after they ate just like Nubby had. Sweet Girl and Dinky had a long journey ahead of them. But Lou and Mark knew they could go on to live great lives. Nubby had taught them that.

Nubby watched Mom and Dad care for the four little puppies who had arrived. They were so tiny. They slept a lot, curled up on a little blanket all snuggled together. And they made squeaking noises. Nubby was used to getting all the attention. But he didn't mind. Rita Rita and his sisters had been nice to him when he first arrived at Hillcrest Manor. He knew he should be nice to these puppies. He'd play with them and care for them just like his sisters had done for him when he was that small. He had plenty of toys to share. He'd teach them how to shake Hedgie until his fluff came out and how *not* to bite the bed. And most importantly, he'd teach those little puppies with two legs how to hop.

By the time they turned eight weeks old in September, Dinky and Sweet Girl were catching up. They were learning how to pop up on their hind legs just like Nubby had when he was their age. They were wagging their tails. They were eating puppy food. They were pooping regularly. And their teeth were finally starting to come in. But most importantly, they were playing! They loved to roll around and bite each other.

"Will they be up for adoption?"

"They are so adorable!"

"The cuteness is slaying me!"

Nubby Nation loved seeing the little pack thrive.

The other dogs of Hillcrest Manor behaved as usual. Rita Rita was ready to play with the pups as soon as they were able. Gracie walked past the little pack daily to check on them and then left. *You're good? Okay, cool.* Maggie ignored them until they had been around for four weeks. Olivia Pig was gentle and let them nip at her while she rested nearby. But the dog who impressed Lou and Mark most was Nubby. He loved the little pack. He was so nurturing to them, and gentle when he played with them. He even broke up fights when they argued over who got to play with the stuffed squirrel.

Nubby grew especially attached to Dinky. They played together inside. They played together outside. They cuddled together on the dog bed. They were inseparable. Dinky could now hop around the living room without a problem, jump on and off his doggy bed, and shake stuffed toys in his mouth like crazy. Even though they were twice his size. "You cannot possibly let Dinky leave! He's perfect for Nubby!" one Nubby Nation follower had said. *Oh no, here we go again*, thought Lou.

Lou knew she would have no problem finding forever homes for Mo and Jules. In fact, she already had homes lined up for them. For Dinky and Sweet Girl, finding the perfect forever home would take more time. It took more time to care for two-legged pups so she needed to find the perfect family who could support and love them. She'd reach out to all the people she knew who rescued dogs and all the people she knew who had dogs with disabilities. Social media made it really easy for her to connect with animal lovers all over the country and find the best families for her rescues. When the right forever home came along, she'd know it in her heart. And when that time came, she'd have to lock her heart away because saying good-bye to rescues never got easier. But she knew it was the right thing to do. *Stick to the mission*, she reminded herself. After the little pack was placed in new homes, she would have more time to rescue the next animal, whoever they may be.

Lou knew that, just like Nubby, these two-leggers would be just fine. Dinky and Sweet Girl would play and move and live happily—all the things Lou and Mark had dreamed of for Nubby when he was that small. And all the things that—against all odds—he had achieved. As she watched the little pack play together, Lou was reminded of their first few months with Nubby: the first time he wagged his tail, or climbed out of his bed, or started chewing toys like crazy with Rita Rita. As well as the first time he had to go to the hospital—and the second time—and how he bounced back again and again. And all the people who were cheering them on and supporting them along the way through his first birthday and on to his second. It was hard to imagine all the members of Nubby Nation who were out there watching and loving on Nubby as much as she and Mark were.

*Wow, has it been a journey*, she thought. Despite all the hard work, Nubby had filled Lou's and Mark's lives with more happiness and hope than they ever could have dreamed. And after all the ups and downs of the past two years, after all the worrying about legs and wheels and body casts and measurements, they knew one thing for sure: Nubby never needed four legs. All he needed was right here at Hillcrest Manor: Olivia Pig, Maggie, Gracie, Rita Rita, and, of course, Lou and Mark. And boy did they need him.

# LOU AND MARK'S RESCUE

W.E.A.R. is a nonprofit animal rescue run by founder, Lou Robinson, with help from her husband, Mark Bowlin, in Conroe, Texas. Its mission is to educate and raise awareness about the care and happiness of pets. By educating the public, W.E.A.R. hopes to change the future for dogs and cats in need, including pets with special needs. In Texas, there is an overpopulation of abandoned, abused, and homeless dogs and cats, but W.E.A.R. hopes to reduce that number. Programs like the Never Lost Pet Project, which microchips local pets for free, help ensure that lost pets will always be reunited with their owners.

Lou loves teaching students from kindergarten through twelfth grade how they can be better friends to their own pets and the animals in their community. She teaches kids how to be a "warrior" for a dog or cat by fighting for what is right for pets and acting as their voice. Nubby sometimes makes a special appearance, especially when Lou is teaching the message "Different is not disposable," because special-needs pets can make great companions, too.

Besides educating the public and advocating for animals in the community, W.E.A.R. also rescues animals in need. Those animals are sometimes special-needs pets and can range from dogs to goats to birds. For more information, ask an adult to search for W.E.A.R. online. And to follow along with Nubby's story, ask an adult to search for "Nubby Dog Rules" on Facebook or Instagram.

# W.E.A.R. WARRIORS

Through W.E.A.R., Lou and Mark have rescued many animals. They couldn't do it without the help of volunteers who act as foster parents. Foster parents care for and home a pet temporarily until the rescue finds the pet a permanent home. This allows Lou and Mark to rescue animals even when they don't have space at Hillcrest Manor. But, of course, Lou and Mark have also personally acted as foster parents to many rescues. Here are just a few.

## LITTLE BABY GOAT

Little Baby Goat was a three-day-old white baby goat whom Lou and Mark rescued. He lived at Hillcrest Manor for only twenty-four hours while they kept him warm and fed. Nubby and Rita Rita loved playing with the soft and fluffy kid and were especially sad to see him go. He found a great home with a family who knew how to bottle-feed baby goats.

## DIGIT

Digit was a brown-and-white French bulldog who came to W.E.A.R. when he was just a little puppy. He had six toes on one foot. As he grew, he couldn't put weight on his back leg. With some extra love and care, his leg strengthened so he could put weight on it and use it for balance. Digit loved to play with the "little pack" of Chihuahuas while he lived at Hillcrest Manor. He went on to find a forever home when he was four months old.

## SCRUFFY

This little puppy, a black-and-white mix, was found on the side of a highway at a construction site. It took three days before she let a human pick her up. She had a dog friend with her who was microchipped. He had been missing for five months but was then reunited with his family. Scruffy entered W.E.A.R. until she could find a forever home. She now lives with a nice man who was looking for a dog friend to love, and she sleeps on a king-sized bed.

## KIMMIE

Kimmie was a three-legged eight-year-old dog found in bad shape on the streets of Houston. Luckily, she was able to get healthy and happy at Hillcrest Manor after a few trips to the vet and a lot of love and care. She especially loved playing with Rita Rita. She moved on to a forever home in Maryland where her new family loves her very much.

## PRINCESS

Princess was a white boxer who was found scooting down a road. Her back legs weren't working, and she was very thin. While getting healthy at Hillcrest Manor, Princess got a wheelchair that held up her back legs so she could walk more easily. She liked to wheel around in the backyard and follow Mark's riding lawn mower. Rita Rita and Nubby took great care of her, and she found a loving forever home soon after.

# WHAT IS AN ANIMAL RESCUE?

Every animal rescue is different, but they all have one goal: to help pets in need find a safe and happy home. These pets were usually abandoned or abused, which means their owners didn't take care of them nicely. The mission of these rescue organizations is to get these homeless pets healthy and happy so they can be adopted into a loving family or live a great life at an animal sanctuary. Rescues will care for the pet until they are healthy and can be placed in a forever home—no matter how long that takes. Rescues really get to know each animal they take in. That means that when you adopt an animal from a rescue organization, they'll have a lot of knowledge about whether your family would be a good fit for the pet, as well as information on the pet's health status.

Some animal rescues are very specialized and take only very specific kinds of animals, or even very specific breeds. It just depends on what kind of animal the founder especially loves or is knowledgeable about. For example, one rescue might focus on baby goats, while another rescue might just be for boxers.

Many rescues are private organizations that are run by animal lovers. They feed the animals and take them to the vet to make sure they have their shots, are neutered or spayed, and are microchipped before they are made available for adoption. The rescuers often rely on donations from other animal lovers and need help from volunteers who can act as foster parents and help get these homeless animals healthy until they can place them in forever homes. Rescue organizations may or may not have a facility that you can visit. Oftentimes, the rescue is run out of someone's home, and that's why they rely on other animal lovers to offer up their homes as foster parents.

Another type of animal rescue is an animal shelter, which is usually public and funded by a town or city. Animal shelters are sometimes very big, and they may even have a building where you can see all the different pets they have for adoption. Because animal shelters take in so many animals, they can't always care for ones who are sick or need extra help. So some shelters partner with smaller, private animal rescues to make sure needy pets get special attention and find homes, too.

## GET INVOLVED!

If you're not able to adopt a pet, your family could consider volunteering as a foster family with a local rescue organization. The rescue will also likely be looking for donations of pet food, blankets, beds, toys, towels, and more. Or they may need an extra hand during an adoption or microchipping event that they are hosting. Ask an adult to search online to find out what your local animal rescue needs. They can search "animal rescue near me" to find a rescue in your town. Make sure the rescue is in good standing by asking an adult to search for it on guidestar.org, which is a listing of 501(c)(3) nonprofit organizations.

# ANIMAL ISSUES

W.E.A.R.'s mission is to better educate people about certain issues that affect the quality of life of dogs and cats. These are some of the ways that pets can live happier, healthier, and safer lives.

## MICROCHIPPING

A microchip is a small device that is inserted into a pet with a needle. (Don't worry, it doesn't hurt much more than a typical shot!) It's a tiny glass capsule, about the size of a grain of rice, and inside it is a microchip. When the microchip is scanned, it displays a number on a screen. That number corresponds to information about who the pet's owner is and how to contact them in case the pet ever gets separated from his or her owner. Every pet should also have a collar and tag with current contact information, but microchips are great since sometimes collars can fall off when a pet gets lost.

When a lost pet is found, a veterinary clinic or animal shelter can scan the microchip and then look up the number in the microchip database. Then they can reunite the pet and the pet owner based on that information. If there was no microchip or updated contact information, the pet would have to go to an animal rescue. But animal rescues are often overcrowded, and if it's a busy shelter, they may only be able to keep a pet for a couple of days before they're put up for adoption. That's not very long to find a missing pet!

If you want to microchip your pet, visit your local veterinarian. They can insert a microchip quickly and easily at your pet's next appointment. Or look for an upcoming microchipping event organized by an animal rescue in your area. Once the microchip is inserted, ask an adult to register the microchip with your latest contact information.

## SPAYING AND NEUTERING

When a dog or cat is spayed or neutered, it means they can't have any babies. When it comes to dogs and cats, this is a good thing! That's because there are so many dogs and cats in the world without homes. It's called overpopulation. There are more pets than there are people who can care for them. This is a big problem!

A veterinarian can easily spay or neuter a pet. Spaying is the procedure that is performed on a female animal and neutering is the procedure that is performed on a male animal. If your pet is healthy and strong, the vet will use anesthesia, which is a shot that helps your pet feel no pain. Then they perform a surgery and finish with some stitches. Your pet will have to rest for a few days but then will be fine. Not only does spaying and neutering help keep pet overpopulation down, but it has other benefits for your pet. It can help reduce behavioral problems, which means your pet will be a better-behaved pet. It can also reduce some serious health problems, like cancer.

## FOSTERING

A foster home is a temporary home. If you decide to foster a pet, you'll be caring for him or her for a short period of time until a permanent home can be found. It could range from two weeks to three months or more. You'll need your time, your love, and pet supplies like food. For a brief period, you'll treat this pet as if they were your own. These pets may have special circumstances, too. For example, a mom cat may need a safe space away from other animals to raise her litter of kittens for a couple of months before they are ready for adoption.

Fostering pets is a big help to rescue organizations that often run out of room. They can't possibly give a temporary home to every animal they find. Foster parents can literally save a pet's life! Although it may be hard to say good-bye when the time comes, seeing them find a loving forever home will make you smile.

## SPECIAL NEEDS

Different is not disposable! That's what Lou teaches through her animal rescue, W.E.A.R. Thanks to Nubby, that message has traveled around the world. Not everyone is willing to adopt a special-needs pet. Special-needs dogs and cats are the hardest pets for rescues to adopt out. They may be deaf, blind, injured, or missing a limb. They may have a disability, a medical issue, or a behavioral issue like being extremely scared of people. But these animals often just need love, time, and training. If someone has the patience to understand their issues and work with them, they can learn how to live their best lives. That's what Lou and Mark did with Nubby. Your veterinarian can always help offer advice and resources if you're considering adopting a special-needs pet.

# PETS AND EMERGENCIES

When Hurricane Harvey struck Houston, Texas, Lou and Mark helped by giving shelter to lost pets or pets whose owners had lost their homes. Natural disasters like bad storms, wildfires, or tornadoes can be hard on families and their pets, especially if they lose power or have to leave their homes temporarily. Here are some ways you can be better prepared when it comes to your pet.

- Pack a pet emergency kit now, so it's readily available in case of an emergency. Keep a three-day supply of pet food in a waterproof container as well as an extra leash, toy, and blanket. Also include medication if your pet needs any.
- Keep your pet's microchip or collar tag up-to-date with your most recent address and phone number.
- If you have to leave your house, don't forget to grab a kennel, or a place to keep your pet contained or safe, as well as a leash. Pets can be just as nervous as you are, and you don't want them to run away in a stressful situation. Putting a blanket over a kennel can help keep your pet calm.
- Make sure you have a recent photo of your pet in case they ever do go missing.

- Try not to leave your pet behind. You can't assume that they will safely survive a disaster. If you're not sure how to transport your pet safely to a different location, call a local animal rescue to ask for help.

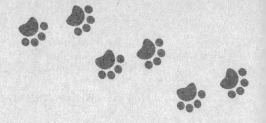

# HOW TO DEAL WITH LOST PETS

**IF YOUR PET GETS LOST**

It's scary when a pet goes missing. Hopefully a microchip and a collar and ID tag with your current contact information will ensure that the two of you are reunited as quickly as possible. But there are additional steps you can take to help make sure your pet finds their way home fast.

1. Ask an adult to call all of the animal shelters within a sixty-mile radius of your

home, including animal control agencies. If you think your pet was stolen, call the police department. Provide everyone with a recent photo and a complete description of your pet.

2. Search your neighborhood every day. This includes driving or walking around the block, visiting local shelters daily, and asking neighbors and community members if they've seen your pet.

3. With an adult's help, pass out or hang up a printout of a recent photograph of your pet and information on how you can be reached. Include details about your pet's color, breed, age, and weight, and any other identifying details.

4. Ask an adult to search lost and found pet databases online such as:

- petfbi.org
- thecenterforlostpets.com
- missionreunite.org

## IF YOU FIND A LOST PET

If you ever see a dog or cat who seems to be missing and there's no owner around, what should you do? Never approach a pet on your own. Ask an adult for help, then follow these steps.

1. Ask an adult to calmly coax the animal closer. Check to see if the pet has an ID tag on their collar with the owner's information. If they do, contact the owner immediately.

2. Secure the pet with a leash (for a dog) or in a large box with air holes (for a cat or other

small animal) while you transport them to safety. If you can't capture the animal safely or if the animal is injured, call your local animal control. Don't let a strange animal loose in a car. It could be dangerous for the driver if the animal gets scared and tries to run or bite.

3. If the animal doesn't have a collar with an ID tag, call a local animal shelter and report the found animal. A local shelter is likely one of the first places a pet owner will call as they search for their missing pet. The shelter will scan the pet for a microchip, which contains the owner's information. If you can't transport the animal to the shelter yourself, call animal control.

4. If there is no ID tag and no microchip, ask

the shelter if it posts photos of found animals online. If they don't, you can help. Ask an adult to post the missing pet's information online. Make and print flyers with the pet's photo on it and hang them near where the animal was found. Consider leaving off one identifying detail that only the true owner would know about their pet, so you can make sure the animal goes home with the right family.

After you've informed the shelter that you've found the pet, consider what you want to do next. If your family can care for the pet, you can keep the animal in your own home as you search for the owner. (Make sure to keep the animal separate from your pets because it could be sick or scared of other animals.) Or you can decide to surrender the pet to a "no kill" shelter or a rescue that will re-home the pet if the owner is not found. Either way, look for "missing pet" posters in your community that the owner may have hung.